Knowing Jesus
Is Everything

Other books by Alejandro Bullón:

The Coming
The Invitation

To order, call 1-800-765-6955.

Visit us at **www.AutumnHousePublishing.com**
for information on other Autumn House® products.

Knowing Jesus Is Everything

Alejandro Bullón

Autumn
House® Publishing
www.autumnhousepublishing.com
A Division of **REVIEW AND HERALD® PUBLISHING**
Since 1861

Published by Autumn House® Publishing, a division of Review and Herald® Publishing, Hagerstown, MD 21741-1119

Autumn House® titles may be purchased in bulk for educational, business, fund-raising, or sales promotional use. For information, please e-mail SpecialMarkets@reviewandherald.com.

Autumn House® Publishing publishes biblically based materials for spiritual, physical, and mental growth and Christian discipleship.

The author assumes full responsibility for the accuracy of all facts and quotations as cited in this book.

This book was
Edited by Gerald Wheeler
Copyedited by James Cavil
Translated by Alice Botelho
Cover designed by Trent Truman
Cover art by Raoul Vitale
Typeset:Bembo 11/14

PRINTED IN U.S.A.

13 12 11 10 09   5 4 3 2 1

Library of Congress Cataloging-in-Publication Data

Bullón, Alejandro, 1947-   .
  Knowing Jesus is everything / Alejandro Bullón.
    p. cm.
  1. Spirituality—Adventists. 2. Christian life—Adventist authors. 3. Jesus Christ—Person and offices. I. Title.
  BV4501.3.B855 2009
  248.8'3—dc22

                                        2008039430

ISBN 978-0-8127-0488-4

Contents

Preface

My conversations with hundreds of young people and the many letters that I constantly receive (some of them dramatic cries of anguished hearts) have encouraged me to write this little book. It is my goal to express in it that which brought peace and joy to my own heart.

I have come to the conclusion that young Christians do not feel happy most the time because they do not understand who Jesus is, what He has done for them, or how to have a personal relationship with Him. Many know what to do and what not to do, but find themselves incapable of living up to the rules. Their many errors leave them feeling constantly distressed. A mysterious inner drive compels them to do what they do not want. One failure follows another, followed by that mortifying whisper: "You are good for nothing—you will never make it. Why do you think you can get by being a hypocrite? It is better to give up religion altogether."

Either such young people abandon the church or remain totally frustrated, feeling as if they are complete failures doomed to living a meaningless life. They may smile outwardly at the world, but they are crying inside. The worst of it is that they may become used to such a situation and accept it as normal. Little by little they begin to ignore God's appeals to them and become lost forever, even while still belonging to the church.

I have written this little book for you, the youth of the church. It was composed not only with ink, but especially with love. For several years I worked with young people, talking with them beside campsite bonfires, in sports fields, at church, in the office—any time of the day. Year after year of listening to their joys, sorrows, victories, and failures prompted me to prepare these pages.

My greatest concern as I wrote was not writing style—it is you. Nor was it the beauty of the language, but to be understood by you. That is all. I am writing as I always spoke with you at camp meetings and revivals, trying to help you, because your problem was mine for several years, and I know exactly the anguish that those feel when they know what the church expects, yet cannot meet it. But above all, I have written it because one day I found Jesus as my great friend and learned that the Christian life is not only a concern with laws and regulations, but is something beautiful—it is walking each day with Jesus in a sublime love relationship.

My most profound desire is that this book may help you to hold on to the hand of this wonderful Person, who will fill your life with peace and happiness. After all, to know Jesus is all.

—Alejandro Bullón

Chapter One

Lost in the Church

Entering the room without knocking, he threw himself in the chair across from my desk. From the way he was sweating, it was clear that he was nervous.

"Pastor, I'm lost!" he said bluntly. Only three words. Nothing else would be necessary to describe the tragedy of a soul in conflict.

I knew that young man very well. We had worked together planning a number of church programs for the youth of the congregation. Now with tearful eyes he kept on repeating: "Believe me, Pastor, I am lost!"

His voice trembling, he told me his story.

"I have been a Seventh-day Adventist since birth. Everyone thinks I'm a good Christian. My parents believe that I'm a wonderful son. The church members consider me a devout Christian. They have even chosen me to be the youth leader. Many times I hear parents telling their children: 'I wish you were like this boy.' Everyone regards me as a model of a Christian, but that is not true. I'm miserable. I just did something horrible, and it was not the first time. The despair and anguish has become so great that I wish I could di. I'm not what other people assume I am."

When I tried to say something, he immediately added, "I do want to be like that. I want to be a genuine Christian, but I can' have tried many times, but I always fail."

My heart ached as I listened.

"You are disappointed with me, aren't you?" he asked anxiou

Disappointed? I was almost crying. But I tried to hide my s ness, my grief, because in reality he was not alone in his predicam

At that moment I saw in that chair many other young people from my church—and perhaps even you.

"Pastor, I am lost!" Lost? Yes, lost in the church. Is it possible to be lost in the church? Unfortunately, yes, it is. Not only are there those who, like this young man, are doing wrong things that nobody sees. There is yet another class of lost people—those who do all that is correct, follow all the church rules, meticulously follow detailed regulations, but are equally lost.

The incident reminds me of the biblical story of the rich ruler in Mark 10. A young man like any other one in the church today, he belonged to a congregation whose leaders were very much concerned with laws and regulations. "Do not do this, don't do that. This is sin, and that is also sin." That ruler grew up with a wrong picture of God. He looked upon Him as sitting with a long face on His throne, dictating rules, rod in hand ready to punish the disobedient.

Since his childhood the man's parents and church leaders had required strict observance of all rules. They were concerned with the image of the church. To update the story, if a girl would wear something unacceptable, for instance, they would take her to the disciplinary committee. Then, loving her church, she would stop wearing whatever it was, and everybody would be happy, without any concern for her feelings. The important thing was to obey the rules—to be a good church member. And thus the rich young ruler learned to observe all laws and regulations. Apparently he was well behaved, active in church programs and serving as a good role model. However, something was wrong in his innermost being. He was not happy, and felt lost in spite of all his faithful observation of the laws.

Then one day he heard that Jesus was coming to his town.

The leaders of the church, always concerned with details and rules, were the first ones to greet Jesus: "Is it lawful for a man to put away his wife?" "Is it a sin to pray while seated?" "Is it wrong for a girl to have short hair?" "Is it wrong to have a recreational center

10

beside the church?" "Is it a sin to go to the beach?" The Lord Jesus did not have time to argue with them. Instead, He received a group of children, took them in His arms, and fondly caressed and kissed their innocent faces.

The scene touched the young ruler. He had never thought that Jesus was capable of relating to children in such a way. This was not what he had been taught about the Son of God. For the first time in his life he felt a desire to open his heart to someone. And when Jesus was leaving the city, he "ran up to him and fell on his knees before him. 'Good teacher,' he asked, 'what must I do to inherit eternal life?' " (Mark 10:17). In reality he was saying: "Good teacher, what must I do to be saved? I am afraid that I'm lost. I am not sure about my salvation."

Wasn't he a good church member? Wasn't he obeying all the commandments? But to keep the law does not mean to be saved. Nor does being a church member in good standing guarantee salvation. It is possible to observe all the rules and yet be totally lost. Yes, lost in the midst of the church!

Jesus tried to make the young ruler understand what he had not yet learned. The man knew the words of the law—the rules—and Jesus told him: "Keep the commandments."

"Lord," he answered confused, "I have observed all of them from my youth." However, he still felt an overwhelming despair, and his sense of being lost increased.

"Jesus looked at him and loved him" (verse 21). Do you want to know something? Jesus loves you, too. It does not matter if you are poor or rich, Black or White, ugly or pretty. He loves you. He understands you. The Bible declares that you are the most important thing to God right now regardless of your troubles, failures, conflicts, doubts, and uncertainties. Even with your crooked character or short temper, you are the object of all His love and compassion. Perhaps sometimes in your life you have had the feeling that nobody loves you, that your parents do not understand you, your teachers do not value you, and that life has denied you the opportunities that others have. Maybe you do not even like or accept yourself. But whether it might be true or not, God still loves you. He understands you. At this very moment, while you are reading this book, He is very near, ready to help you, to value you.

There centuries ago beyond the Jordan Jesus beheld the rich young ruler and loved him. He saw his inner conflicts, his battles, his anguish, his desperate situation of being lost in the church while observing all the laws and obeying all regulations.

"Son, do you know what your problem is?" Jesus asked. "You do not love Me. In your heart there is no place for Me, only for money. You are willing to observe the commandments, but you do not love Me. If you do not love Me, you are only obeying the letter of the law. Because this does not make any sense, you will continue with that terrible vacuum in your heart. Let us do something, my dear son. Go home now, take your love away from the things of this world, place Me at the center of your life, then come back and follow Me."

The Bible says: "He went away sad, because he had great wealth" (verse 22). What a shame! He was more willing to keep commandments than to love the Lord Jesus. Why? Perhaps it is easier to look good than to surrender the heart to God.

Maybe you are thinking, *I am glad I'm not rich.* But sometimes we do not need to have riches in order to keep Jesus away from our heart. Is it possible that I love a TV artist more than I do Jesus? Is it possible that sports, friends, profession, education—things that in themselves are good—might take the place of Jesus in my heart? Could I love my church, its doctrines and name, more than the Lord Jesus?

Let me ask you: Which should be our first concern—to love Jesus or to observe rules? Sometimes we adults are more concerned that the young obey the rules than that they love Jesus. Jesus has a different interest: "My son, give Me your heart," He declares while knocking at the door of the human heart.

Never should we forget that it is possible to obey the rules without loving Jesus, but that it is impossible to love Jesus and not obey the rules. So what should be our first interest, our main goal? If people love Jesus with all their heart, they will not do anything that hurts their Redeemer. Consequently, their lives will be ones of obedience.

Do you know why so many are not happy in the church? Lack of love for Jesus. Perhaps we are in the church because we love it, its doctrine has convinced us, and the pastor made an overwhelming altar call. Some of us are in the church because our parents want us there, or we want to please our children or spouse, or just because every human being needs a religion, but not because we love Jesus to the point that we can say: "I can't live without You."

"Pastor," an elderly woman told me once, "I have been married for almost 60 years. You may ask my husband, and he will say that I have always been a perfect wife. I have done all that a good wife must do, have always acted properly, but I have never been happy. Why? I do not love my husband, Pastor."

"But why did you marry him?"

"When I was a young girl," she explained, "we did not choose a husband. Our parents did it. One day my father said: 'My daughter, two months from today you will marry the son of one of my best friends.' They prepared my hope chest. The party was ready, and two days before the wedding I met my fiancé. I did not like him. I never could love him, but I got married, because I had to obey. I have been a perfect wife, but never a happy one."

How can we be happy together with someone we do not love? Perhaps we might compare baptism to a marriage ceremony with Christ. Many Christians perhaps could say: "Lord, I am in the church, baptized five, or 10, or 15 years ago. All this time, somehow I have done whatever the church requires. But I have never been happy." Why? Because it is impossible to be happy in the company of someone that we do not love. When living together with someone that we do love is not an easy thing, imagine what it would be like without any love at all. We can never be happy in the church just because we have belonged to it since birth, or because of social, religious, or family pressure. None of these reasons will make any sense unless you have love for Jesus. Otherwise the Christian life will become "hell," a terrible burden to endure. To practice something just because we are baptized, or to obey a few rules just to please someone, is the worst thing that can happen. Always we will find ourselves thinking of some way to get out of it, of forsaking everything. If we think that nobody will see it, we will do something wrong.

All the church rules, all that we have to give up, all that we have to learn, will have meaning only when Christ's love motivates our heart. Our first prayer should not be "Lord, help me to keep Your commandments" but "Lord, help me to love You—with my whole heart."

The rich young ruler went away with a sad heart and never returned. He was willing to be a church member, but not to surrender his heart to the Master.

Chapter Two

The Indian Guide

I guess it was about 3:00 or 4:00 in the afternoon, but in the deep jungle it seemed like twilight. Suddenly black clouds covered the sky and thunder echoed in the immensity of the Amazon forest like the cries of frightened giants. Every few minutes lightning flashed, breaking through the dark sky. I was scared. In fact, I had been frightened since the moment that I noticed that I had lost the trail.

I was a missionary among the Campa Indians, who live along the banks of the Perené River in the Amazon region of my native country. That morning in 1972 I had left my home hoping to visit a village a two-hour walk through the forest. I could not recall the exact moment I lost the trail. But when I tried to find it again, all my efforts only increased my confusion. The minutes and hours slipped away, and then thick clouds announced the approaching storm.

Heavy rain and darkness arrived at the same moment. I sat on the ground under a tree, pleading with God to help me find the trail. I do not know for how long I was there, but when the rain decreased I started walking again through the mud and dark. I was totally wet, tired, hungry, and at that moment almost in despair. "You can't stop—you have to go on," I repeated to myself. "You will find the village—you can't stop."

However, something seemed to argue in my mind that it was useless to continue on, that it would be better to stay there and wait for dawn. Stay there? Soaked from head to toe? Alone? What if some wild animal would come? It was the first time that this had happened to me. I did not know the jungle, having come from the city just a few months earlier. Terror soon overwhelmed me, and I started running insanely, as if someone were after me. The rain blurred my vision, even though I wasn't I able to see very much in such darkness. It was then that I fell down a 15- to 18-foot embankment. Mud covered me from head to foot. There was no sign of any trail. Only darkness and the dreadful pounding of rain on the leaves and ground.

Although I did not want to accept the fact, I was completely lost. When I tried to get out of that hole by grabbing a small tree, it pulled out by the roots, and I slid back into the mud. As I grabbed another one, excruciating pain forced me to release it, and again I splashed back into the mud, my hand full of thorns. Everything I tried was useless. My feet would slip, and back to the bottom of the hole I would go. I felt at the point of tears. Was it because of fear of some wild animal? exhaustion? hunger? I wish it had been only those reasons. But it was not so.

Looking back, I saw that my Christian life had been like that night. All the time trying to get up, to follow all the rules and commandments, yet always finding myself trapped in the same place. I was lost in the church—observing, to a certain extent, all the rules, but still lost. And the worst part of it was that I had been a minister for two years.

Like a movie, my whole life began to unreel before my eyes as I huddled in that jungle hole. My mother had been converted when I was 4 years old. I cannot recall her missing a single meeting. Saturdays, Sundays, and Wednesdays—she was always there with all of us children. Above the rostrum of the little room in which the group of eight people gathered to worship was a very special place for a picture of the Ten Commandments. We all had to know them by memory and keep them faithfully. Since my childhood I had learned all the church rules. No smoking. no drinking, no dancing, no movies—no, no.

"O Lord," I asked myself many times, "how is it possible to live this way?" In my adolescent years I felt a terrible conflict. I knew all that I should do and all that I shouldn't, but, unable to live up to the rules, I was constantly unhappy. I remember a Sabbath that a professional soccer team played in our city. My brother and I left the church meeting to watch the game. Afterward I felt miserable about what I had done. I thought God was going to kill me—that I had lost heaven forever.

At the age of 13 I was baptized, and then my conflict increased. "Now," I repeated to myself, "you are a baptized member, and you cannot do foolish things anymore." However, there was always something wrong with me. Unfortunately, I could not define exactly what it was. I prayed more and more, but it seemed to me that God was far away. That He could never hear me. I read the Bible as a duty. When I turned 15, I read the book *Messages to Young People* and felt myself a greater sinner than ever. *I will never go to heaven,* I thought. *It is impossible to live at such a lofty level.* Only God knows how many times I would lie down and suffer alone in despair. The idea of a God always angry, always ready to punish me, expecting that I should keep all His rules, was a terrible torment.

When I finished high school, I went to college, and my conflict only worsened. "You are a future minister, so you can't make any mistakes. You have to observe every rule," I kept telling myself. Many times I struggled with the idea of abandoning not only school but also the church and my home. Today I thank God that somehow I did not do it.

At 21 I graduated from college, having accomplished not only my mother's dream but also my own. But instead of being happy, I was distressed. "God, what is going on with me? Why do I always think that I'm wrong?" I begged. But I received no answer, and my internal conflict intensified. "Now you are a minister," I repeated, "and you must be an example to the church. Someone needs to keep all the rules, and you are that someone."

The first years of my ministry were very sad. Not that I was a great sinner. One could classify my sins as "tolerables." They were minor errors. But I realized that God does not classify sins, and that fact tortured me. I knew the doctrine of Christ. I knew all the church rules by heart, and also hundreds of Bible texts. In church I preached about Jesus and would then go back home feeling distressed. All day long the rules dominated my mind. Constantly I thought about what to do and what not to do. My anguish never ceased. In spite of all this, God was extremely kind to me and blessed my ministry during those two years, adding a good number of members to the church.

That night in the jungle, drenched and covered with mud, I understood for the first time what was going on with me. I was lost in a jungle of doctrines, rules, laws, and theology. Lost in the church!

I looked around me in the darkness. Where was the Jesus that I preached about? He was far away, beyond the clouds. In my mind was only theory, rules, and doctrines. I cried—cried like a baby, because I felt loneliness. I knew a name, not a person. I loved a church, but not the wonderful Lord of the church. I kept rules and laws, but I did not have Jesus. And in that moment I did not need rules or doctrines—I needed a Person. I cried that night for the tragedy of a lonely life— trying to get out of the hole but always falling back in the mud.

The rain began to decrease. *A miracle,* I thought. *I need a miracle to get out of this place.* Then I started shouting with all my strength. In the forest when someone is lost, it is necessary to shout. If another person hears, they will shout back in response, and thus help will come.

Suddenly I heard a distant voice. I shouted again. My voice vanished in the immensity of the jungle, and the wind brought the answer. Somebody was there. I kept on shouting, and the voice came nearer and nearer. Soon I heard his footsteps and then noticed his silhouette. As he neared I saw his face—he was an Indian. Stretching out his arm, he took my hand and pulled me up. His hand was strong and calloused, and he tugged until I was out. "Who are you?" I asked. He did not answer. "What is your name?" No answer. "Where did you come from?" Silence. Gripping me by my arm, he started walking.

We continued in silence for a time. Before long I could see some lights. It was the place I had been looking for when I had gotten lost. I was safe! Leaving the Indian, I started running in the forest till I slipped and fell. Again he stretched out his arm, seized my hand, and took me to the shack where the light was shining.

John came to the door holding a torch.

"Pastor," he exclaimed, "how did you arrive at this hour?"

"I lost the trail," I answered as I took off my wet clothes, laid them near the fire, and fell asleep.

When I woke up the next morning, I noticed three things: my clothes were dry near the fire, my bag rested a little farther way, and there was manioc (a starchy root) for me to eat and "chapo" (a drink from cooked platanos) to drink. A few minutes later John arrived.

"How did you find the trail?" he asked.

"It was the Indian," I answered.

"Which Indian?"

"The one who was with me last night when I got here."

Puzzled, he said, "There was no Indian with you last night."

I did not say a word. Leaving John there, I walked to a small waterfall to wash myself. There I dropped to my knees as I heard the musical sound of the water splashing on the rocks and the birds singing, and said: "Lord Jesus, now I know that You are not a doctrine; You are a wonderful person. How could I walk alone all my life? Oh, Lord, now I know why I was not happy. I did not have You. Now I want to love You. I want to hold Your all-powerful arm. I know that I am lost without You. From now on I want to have You by my side. I know You are not only in heaven but here with me. Today I understand what was missing. It was You, dear Jesus."

Since that day I have regarded the Christian living not as a heavy set of rules and regulations, but as the wonderful experience of walking with Jesus. All that was meaningless before now made sense as I saw the beauty of Jesus. I never tried to discover if that Indian was a real human being or an angel. It was not important. That night I learned the greatest lesson of my life. All by myself I would be lost, distressed, unhappy. I needed the help of a powerful friend. This friend I found in Jesus, and for that reason I will be forever thankful to You, O God!

Chapter Three

How Could You Not Love Him?

D addy, why should I love Jesus?" one of my sons asked me one day. Trying to find an answer that would satisfy his curiosity, I looked him in the face and asked, "Do you love Daddy?"

"Of course I do."

"But did you ever think why you love Daddy?"

His little eyes quickly glanced from one side to the other, and with a big smile brightening his face he said, "Because you love me."

Love has the amazing power to captivate, because love generates love. Nobody is able to resist its magnetic power, and one of the great biblical truths is that Jesus loved us in such a way that the least we can do is love Him in return. But why do human beings seem incapable of loving God? Sometimes it is because we do not understand what He has done for us. We constantly repeat that He died on the cross to save us, but I am afraid that we really do not know what that means. Having heard it so many times since childhood, we have probably lost sight of the concept's real meaning.

A few years ago in the college in which I studied, I witnessed a beautiful love story. One of the most plain students married one of the most pretty girls. She was a freshman that year. The most handsome, smart, and outgoing guys had repeatedly approached her without success.

One day a friend came to see me and announced, "I have a problem."

"What is it?"

"I am in love."

"Congratulations! This is something great—not a problem at all."

"Wait a minute. I am talking about *that* particular girl."

I stopped smiling and, almost whispering, replied, "She has totally ignored the best-looking guys on campus. Do you think she is going to notice you?"

"I know," he answered sadly. "I know it, but what can I do if I love her?"

The months went by, and love silently continued to grow in his heart. By the end of the first semester rumors began to circulate that she would not return, because of lack of money to pay her tuition.

My friend went to see the administrator, offering to pay her expenses with the money he had earned selling books. It meant that he would have to miss one school year and sell more books in order to continue his studies.

The administrator tried to dissuade him, but did not succeed. "It is my money, and I want to pay her tuition. But please keep it confidential."

Thus he left school for one year to sell more books in order to finance his next school term.

A few months later I received a letter from him. "You say that my sacrifice is useless, that she will never care for me. Anyway, I love her, and I could not bear the idea of seeing her missing school for lack of money. I am happy just doing it, even if she will never look at me."

The next year he returned. His love had intensified to the point that he had gathered enough courage to declare it. It was a sad moment. She not only refused to accept it, but actually despised him. It was then that a friend approached her and said, "Listen, you have the right to say no to him, but you should be more polite. You did not have to hurt him. It is true that he is not very handsome, is not very athletic, but he loves you to the point that last year he dropped out of school so that you could stay here, and he did it secretly, just because he loves you."

Shocked, the girl began to cry. She asked the school administration if it was true. After she learned that it was, she felt even more humiliated.

Months later my friend announced, "We are dating!"

Everyone thought, *It is simply because she feels sorry for him.* But one day she said something beautiful. "When I learned what he had done for me, I felt hurt, even offended. But after a time, when I had calmed down, I asked myself, 'Would it be possible for me to find another boy on this earth who loves me to the point of sacrificing one year of his studies, hoping for no reward, wishing that I would not know what he was doing?' Then I concluded: How could I not love someone who loves me so?"

"How could I not love someone who loves me so?"

When we really understand what happened that day in the cross at Calvary, there is no doubt that we will come to the same conclusion the girl came to.

But what happened there?

Let us go back to the Garden of Eden. After God created the first human being, "the Lord God commanded the man, 'You are free to eat from any tree in the garden; but you must not eat from the tree of the knowledge of good and evil, for when you eat of it you will surely die'" (Gen. 2:16, 17). In other words, obedience brings life, and disobedience leads to death. The human race sinned, and consequently has to die. "For the wages of sin is death" (Rom. 6:23). But the human being who does not want to die asks forgiveness. "God, forgive me," he or she pleads. Do you know what the person is trying to say? "Father, I have sinned and deserve death, but I do not want to die." Such a supplication creates a conflict, because God's word is immutable. The consequence of sin is death, but God loves humanity and does not want it to perish. Something has to be done. Where there is sin, there is death, "and without the shedding of blood there is no forgiveness" (Heb. 9:22).

Someone has to pay the price so that the human race will not have to perish. It is then that God the Son says: "Father, humanity deserves to die, because they have sinned, but before they pay the penalty, I want go to the earth as a human being and live as they do. I want to take their nature, experience their conflicts, sorrows, joys, and temptations." It was for that reason that Christ came to our world as an infant.

He not only looked human; He was a real human. The same as you and I. Jesus endured the same trials that you have, and He felt lonely and many times misunderstood, as you do. Jesus experienced your temptations, and that's why—not just because He is God—He is more willing to love and understand you than to judge and condemn.

The Lord Jesus lived on earth 33 years. The Bible says that He "has been tempted in every way, just as we are—yet was without sin" (Heb. 4:15). Well, if He lived in our world as a human being, and was tempted as a human being, but did not sin, He deserves to live.

Now let us imagine a conversation between Jesus and His Father.

"Father, I lived on earth as a human being, and I was tempted but did not sin. As a result I have the right to live. The human race, on the contrary, sinned and deserves death. So the death that it deserves, I want to take upon Me; and the life that I deserve, since I have not sinned, I want to offer to humanity."

That is what happened on the cross of Calvary. An exchange based on love. Someone died in our place. Someone died to save us.

A few days before Christ's death the authorities in Jerusalem arrested a criminal named Barabbas. They judged and condemned him to death. He was to be crucified, a cruel form of death. Nobody immediately dies because of wounds on the hands or feet. Death on the cross is slow. Sometimes the condemned victim would hang on the cross for several days, enduring the heat of the day and the cold of the night, hungry, thirsty, losing blood very slowly, until his life slipped away.

After the judgment and sentence, the authorities summoned a carpenter to make a cross for Barabbas. The condemned criminal was there, and so was the cross. It had been made especially for him, carefully measured and bearing his name. But on that day the Jewish leaders also arrested Jesus and judged and condemned Him. The Roman official Pilate, trying to defend Jesus, presented Him and Barabbas to the people and said, "During festive days it is a custom to release a prisoner. Whom do you want me to release this time: Christ or Barabbas?"

And the crazy multitude shouted, "Release Barabbas! Crucify Christ!"

I guess that if anyone ever understood completely the meaning of the expression "Christ died in my place," it was Barabbas. He could hardly believe his fate. Perhaps he even pinched himself to verify that he was not dreaming. He, the criminal, was free. And Jesus, meek and gentle, sharing love all the time, restoring health to the sick and life to the dead, was there to die in his place. I like to imagine that Barabbas thought to himself: *I will never have words to thank Jesus for being here just now. If He had not come, I would be irrevocably condemned.*

The authorities had no time to summon a carpenter to prepare a cross especially for Jesus. But they did have an empty cross, measured and prepared for someone else, bearing another name. That day, my dear young people, Jesus carried to Calvary someone else's cross, because no one ever prepared a cross for Him. Do you know why? Because He did not deserve a cross. That day Christ was carrying my cross. I was the one who deserved to die, but He loved me in such a way that He decided to die for me and offer me the right to live a life that He, as a man, had won.

Finally the soldiers arrived at the execution site. They laid the cross on the ground, and with big nails piercing His hands and feet, they secured Him to the cross. As they lifted the wooden beam, the weight of His body tore His flesh. One soldier had placed a crown of thorns on His head. Blood slowly ran down His face. There hung the Man-God dying because He loved. The sun stopped shedding its light, as if to hide the agony of that moment. Even the birds and wild animals seemed to sense that something strange was happening. Only humanity, the most noble and intelligent of God's earthly creatures, appeared unaware that its eternal destiny was at stake just then.

A few hours later, after many of the Jewish leaders had returned home, the wonderful Jesus endured the most intense agony while giving His life for humanity.

Did you ever stop to think of the meaning of this act of love?

It was not a crazy suicide who died on the cross. Nor was it a social revolutionary who paid the price for his beliefs. It was God in the likeness of a man, and as a man He feared death. In fact, the night before His crucifixion He said to His Father as He prayed in Gethsemane, "Father, I'm afraid to die. If there is another way to save the world—if I do not have to go through this trial—I will be very grateful" (see Luke 22:42).

And I want to believe that God answered, "There is time yet to change Your mind, My Son."

The destiny of all humanity rested in His hands. He was afraid to die, but His love was greater than His fears. How could He abandon humanity to despair and death? That is what I may never be able to understand. Why did He love me so? Do you understand the significance of your life? You are the most important thing that Christ has. He loves you to the point that even being afraid to die, He did so just to see you happy—not only a happy church member, but a happy person.

Pastor H.M.S. Richards tells us a story of his childhood. He says that he liked to climb over the fence and pick apples from the neighbor's orchard. One day his mother called him and, showing him a switch, said, "Do you see this stick?"

"Yes, Mother."

"If you get one more apple from our neighbor, I am going to

spank you five times with it. Understand?"

"Yes, Mother."

A few days went by. The apples were getting redder, and the boy could not resist the temptation. Scrambling over the fence, he ate as many apples as he could. But he did not think that when he returned, his mother would be there waiting with the switch in her hand. Trembling, he knew what was going to happen. Without a second thought he begged, "Forgive me, Mother."

"No, son—I have to do what I told you."

"Mother, please, I promise that I will never do it again."

"I can't, son. You must be punished."

"Please, Mother, please!" he repeated, tears in his eyes.

Could a mother not be touched by the supplications of her beloved child? Taking his hands in hers, she asked, "You do not want to suffer the consequences?"

"No, Mother."

"Well, then there is only one solution."

"What is it?"

The mother gave him the switch. "Hold it, son. You spank me, because the punishment has to be done. You do not want to be punished, but I love you so much that I am willing to get punished in your place."

"Until that moment I had cried with my eyes," Richards says, "but after it I cried with my heart. How could I spank my mother for my wrongdoing?"

Did you get the message?

That's what happens between God and us when, after we have sinned, we ask forgiveness. God looks to us and says, "My child, you have sinned, and the consequence is death. But you do not want to die. There is only one alternative."

"What is that?" you ask anxiously.

"You will not have to die for your sins, because I am willing to suffer the consequences for you," He answers in His lovely voice.

Richards did not have the courage to punish his mother for his error. But we had the courage to crucify the Lord Jesus on the cross of Calvary. Every day we "crucify" Him with our acts. And He does not say a word. "He was led like a lamb to the slaughter, and as a sheep before her shearers is silent, so he did not open his mouth" (Isa. 53:7). He does not complain, does not seek His rights. Nor does He think about just retribution. Instead, He only dies, consumed by the flames of a mysterious, incomprehensible, and infinite love.

I will never have adequate words to express my gratitude for what He did for me. Nor will I ever grasp the scope of His love for me. But when I look back to a God of love hanging on a cross, my heart is touched, and as did that college girl, I exclaim:

"How could I not love someone who loves me so?"

Chapter Four

Miracles Are Not Explained—
They Are Accepted

Why is it hard to love God even knowing what He did for us? In John 3 we read the story of a man who could not love in spite of his great knowledge of the Scriptures. Apparently he observed all the rules and tried to be a good church member. Although he held a position of responsibility, he was not happy. Something was missing in his life. The worst part of it was that he could not define what it was.

It is possible that Nicodemus would lie awake several hours during the night, trying to sleep. Maybe he asked many times, "My God, what else do I need? I pay my tithes, I keep the Sabbath, I do missionary work, sing in the choir, teach a Bible class, but I feel that something is wrong with me. It seems that all my efforts are useless. What is happening with me?"

Perhaps it was during one of those sleepless nights that he got up and went out looking for Jesus. He knew where to find Him. After all, he had studied the prophecies, and every one of them indicated clearly that Jesus was the promised Messiah. His problem was not lack of knowledge. Nicodemus' tragedy was that he had never met Jesus personally.

Protected by the darkness, he made his way to where Jesus was. In reality he was embarrassed that other people might see him seeking help. After all, he was a church leader. And leaders are supposed to help, not to ask for it. Do you perceive his predicament? Full of theory, doctrines, prophecies, yet alone and distressed, needing help, but because of his "status" incapable of running as did the rich young ruler and kneeling at Jesus' feet to declare: "Lord, I am lost! What shall I do to be saved?"

It was not difficult for Nicodemus to find Jesus. Christ was on the Mount of Olives, waiting with outstretched arms. Their eyes met. It was an encounter of peace with despair, tranquillity with anguish, certainty with uncertainty.

Jesus saw into Nicodemus' soul, and Nicodemus beheld the great love and kindness in Jesus' heart. He tried to "open his heart" and tell Jesus about his troubles, his failures, his confusion and doubts, but he couldn't. His pride spoke louder.

"Rabbi," he said, "we know you are a teacher who has come from God. For no one could perform the miraculous signs you are doing if God were not with him" (John 3:2).

I think that in reality he wanted to say: "I recognize that You are a master (or teacher), and I came to talk with You as a teacher also. Let us take a look into the prophecies and see how they relate to the things You are doing." Jesus kept on gazing into Nicodemus' eyes, and saw his anguish. He recognized that the religious leader did not need prophecy, theology, or doctrines. Sometimes we human beings get too concerned about theological knowledge when our real necessity is something else.

"Nicodemus," Christ declared, "you must be born again. You must experience conversion. This is your problem, and until you experience rebirth, all your religious practices avail nothing. Nothing can substitute for the experience of conversion."

The statement hit the religious leader like a physical blow.

"How can a man be born when he is old? Can he enter the second time into his mother's womb, and be born?" he asked, implying that he had not understood.

And Jesus, with sadness in His eyes, replied, "Don't pretend, son. You understood perfectly what I meant. I'm talking about conversion, because this is the starting point of a life of happiness. All you have is a head full of theory, rules, and laws, and you feel frustrated because you can't live up to all those regulations. Tonight, my dear son, I want to change you completely, yet you try to hide yourself behind a wall of prejudice and irony."

The story of Nicodemus does not conclude in John 3, because that night he did not respond to Jesus' invitation. It was too hard for him—Nicodemus the leader, theologian, and good church member—to accept that he was not converted. He went away as empty as he had come.

Would you believe me if I told you that his problem is our problem also? Maybe we think that because our name is on the church books (because of baptism), that we are converted. But that is not always the case. We must not confuse conversion with conviction. Both words may sound alike, but they have a totally different meaning. The first deals with heart or life, while the second involves only your intellect. Perhaps someone has come to our home to give us Bible studies. We accept the various doctrines and decide to be baptized. As we emerge from the water we think: "I'm converted now." But it may not be true. Yes, we might be convinced of the doctrines, but that does not mean that we are converted. And there is where confusion starts. We go on living like Nicodemus, perhaps because we were born in a Christian home—but we do so with a sensation of emptiness and failure. We want to love God, but we are incapable of actually doing it. Why?

For us to understand the subject of conversion better, we again have to go back in history and see what happened in the Garden of Eden. There we see the newly created Adam and Eve. The first human pair was perfect, without any tendency toward sin, and fully capable of obeying. The couple delighted in obedience. It was as easy for them to obey as it was to breathe the air. They did not have to try to obey. Their nature was perfect.

The problem started when they sinned, because in that very moment they lost their perfect nature and acquired a strange one incapable of obeying and inclined to finding pleasure in the wrong things. We shall call that the sinful nature.

Now, trapped in their sinful nature, human beings could no longer obey. Instead, to do wrong was as easy as it was to breathe. Unfortunately their sinful nature passed from generation to generation and to all human beings. We are born with this nature, and thus incapable of obedience.

For this reason the Bible says: "Can the Ethiopian change his skin or the leopard its spots? Neither can you do good who are accustomed to doing evil (Jer. 13:23). "The heart is deceitful above all things and beyond cure. Who can understand it?" (Jer. 17:9). "For out of the heart come evil thoughts, murder, adultery, sexual immorality, theft, false testimony, slander" (Matt. 15:19).

"Pastor," you might ask, "do you mean that I will never be able to obey?"

"The way you were born," I answer, "with your sinful nature— no."

This is what Jesus tried to tell Nicodemus when He said, "No one can see the kingdom of God unless he is born again."

George E. Vandeman presented an interesting illustration. Let us suppose, he suggested, that a timber wolf, after watching and admiring the habits of a flock of peaceful sheep, decided that all animals should live in a similar manner. The wolf then attempted to live just as a sheep does. Wouldn't that wolf have a difficult time? Wouldn't it be likely to slip back into its old way of life? Grass might seem quite tasteless as it remembered devouring some carcass.

Also, suppose that the creature did not want to abandon its resolution. Do you think that even five or 10 years later it would enjoy eating grass? Surely not, because it was a wolf, with that animal's inherent nature.

At first the wolf tries very hard to live like a sheep, even though everything a sheep does is contrary to a wolf's nature. As time passes, the wolf's enthusiasm decreases until finally after one or two years it can't resist its wolfish nature any longer. One day while the flock is sleeping it quietly gets up and runs away.

Once away from the sheep, it discards the sheepskin and lives as a wolf, doing all that wolves like to do. Then on the Sabbath it again wraps itself in the sheepskin and goes to church with the sheep, pretending that nothing wrong has happened. However, it knows better, and shame sweeps over the wolf.

Eventually tired of such duplicity, it implores God, "You know that I want to be a real sheep, but You know that I was born a wolf. Please do something to change my nature." And God, by a miracle known only to the Creator, transplants into the wolf the nature of a sheep. Then would it be difficult for the creature to live like a sheep? Not at all!

That's exactly what God promises to us. "I will sprinkle clean water on you, and you will be clean; I will cleanse you from all your impurities and from all your idols. I will give you a new heart and put a new spirit in you" (Eze. 36:25, 26). Peter adds: "Through these he has given us his very great and precious promises, so that through them you may participate in the divine nature and escape the corruption in the world caused by evil desires" (2 Peter 1:4).

Do you understand, my friend? God is promising to give us a new nature, the nature of Christ Himself—one that loves Jesus and finds delight in obedience.

This is conversion. Ellen G. White explains this way: "Of ourselves we are no more capable of living a holy life than was the impotent man capable of walking. There are many who realize their helplessness, and who long for that spiritual life which will bring them into harmony with God; they are vainly striving to obtain it. In despair they cry, 'O wretched man that I am! who shall deliver me from this body of death?' Let these desponding, struggling ones look up" (*The Desire of Ages,* p. 203).

"No one sees the hand that lifts the burden, or beholds the light descend from the courts above. The blessing comes when by faith the soul surrenders itself to God. Then that power which no human eye can see creates a new being in the image of God" (*ibid.*, p. 173).

A new being capable of loving and obeying and who delights to do the will of God. Isn't that a wonderful promise? No one sees the miracle, however, because the promise is from God, not from human beings.

We need to understand one vital thing before we proceed any further. Not all conversions happen the same way. In some cases it is a matter of seconds; other times it is gradual and slow. Great emotion may accompany some conversions, while others may not have any at all. The one is not necessarily more genuine than the other. Some Christians can look back to the exact day and hour it happened. Others are not able to pinpoint the time. Not all persons need the same experience. What matters is that the nature is changed, that the wolf becomes a lamb.

During the first year of my ministry I worked in the ghetto of the capital city of my country. Though the poorest and most neglected people thronged it, it became the scene of some of the most wonderful conversions wrought by the work of the Holy Spirit.

One day, as I walked through the alleys of that neighborhood, a dog started barking at me. Being inexperienced with dogs, I began to run, and in a matter of a few seconds several dogs were barking and racing after me. Scared and trying to hide from the dogs, I pushed open the door of a house. When I noticed where I was, I decided that I would rather have the dogs attacking me. The room was dark and had very little ventilation. Two candles in the center of a table struggled to give off some light. A terrible odor permeated the room. On top of the table was a pile of cigarette butts and coca leaves. Around the table sat some drunk women, and empty bottles littered the floor.

Before I could even offer some explanation, they crowded all around me. I apologized and tried to explain why I had come inside. But they ignored my apologies, and I had to forget my good manners in order to get away from that house.

A few days when I again passed through the area, one of the

women spotted and approached me. "Are you the one who entered our house the other day to get away from the dogs?"

"Yes," I answered, and once more I apologized.

"You do not have to apologize," she said, a little bit surprised. "We ladies are the ones who should ask you to forgive us."

Explaining that I was a minister, and that every night I was conducting a series of religious meetings in a hall on top of the hill, I invited her to attend them.

That same night, to my surprise, she came, though she was drunk and slept all the time. The next night she appeared again, and the next, and the next. Always drunk and always sleeping while I preached.

A few days later she visited me. "Pastor," she said with some emotion and still smelling of alcohol, "I need to talk with you. My life has been a tragedy. You may think that because I am always drunk, I don't understand what you say every night, but I do, and I am in a desperate situation."

I looked at her with sympathy. It was easy to see in her expression the tragedy of a life without Christ. She was almost an incurable alcoholic.

"Pastor," she continued, "I had a beautiful family, a very hardworking and honest husband, and wonderful children. We were never rich, but we always had food on our table until the day that I became an addict. I do not know how it happened. I got to the point that drinking was the most important thing for me. Many times my husband would arrive home, tired after a day of work, only to find me drunk and the children hungry and abandoned. Before long, life at home became unbearable. One day, while my husband was at work, I gathered my clothes and left my home, my husband, and my children, including the baby, who was just 2 years old. I came to this area, and to survive I became a prostitute."

It hurts a lot to see how sin can damage a life, and how it compels a person to do things beyond their comprehension.

"All this time that I have been attending the meetings," she continued, "I have felt that my life cannot go on the way it has been. I have to stop drinking. But when I'm sober, I remember my children and my husband, and then I feel such terrible anguish, so to forget the situation I drink again. My life has become a vicious cycle."

God has promised to make us free, to give us a new nature. He is able to transform our heart. And this is what happened to that woman. From the bottom of the pit of despair and guilt, from the depths of misery and anguish, she cried out to God: "O Lord, change my life, change the direction of my ways, give me freedom from my enslaving vice—give me a new heart."

And God heard her prayer. Nobody saw how it happened, but God's power created a new creature. She stopped drinking, but her lonely life was very sad. It was then that I decided to find her husband. A wonderful man, he had to get up very early in the morning every day to prepare food for himself and the children, and then go to work. The oldest son, a 12-year-old, warmed the food for the younger brothers. In the evening the father returned exhausted, but still cleaned the house and did the laundry. Life was hard.

At first I did not mention a word about his wife. But after a few visits I said that I had come as her representative. His expression changed. Angrily he said, "Do not mention her name again. She ruined my life and my children's lives. In fact, she practically killed us, because to live this way is almost worse than to be dead."

The days went by, and we became good friends. I told him that the woman who had abandoned him was dead, that today she was another woman who did not drink and who was suffering for her wrong deeds.

Whatever is impossible for humanity is possible by the Holy Spirit. A few months later he consented to see his wife. We arranged a time. That night I prayed to God, asking Him for another miracle—that He would touch the husband's heart and reestablish a home broken because of sin. In life we encounter moments that are forever poignant and unforgettable. That night I experienced one of them. As the husband stood with the children around him, the woman approached and fell at his feet.

"Forgive me!" she said in tears. "Forgive me. I do not deserve it, but please, forgive me. I know I do not have any rights—I'm nobody. I just want to take care of you. I will be a servant. I will not complain of anything. I just want be with you and do what I should have done in the past."

As she spoke I kept praying silently in my heart.

All of a sudden the man lifted her by the hand and asked, "Did you stop drinking?"

"Yes. Christ took away my vice a few months ago."

"It is unbelievable!" the husband said with some emotion. "When the pastor told me that you had stopped drinking, I did not believe it, and I wanted to verify it for myself. Now I see that you do not drink anymore. Did you say it was Christ who took away your vice? If it is true, then I want to know this Christ who was able to perform this miracle."

At that moment I turned away to hide my tears, and quietly left the place.

Several months later I had the pleasure of seeing that man, his wife, and their oldest son be baptized.

How does God change a human being? I do not know. But I do know that He is capable of doing it. During the years of my ministry I have seen many lives transformed. Castaways, drug pushers, men and women without any hope. And if God is capable of changing them, isn't He able to change us, too?

"Pastor," you might say, "I am not like the people you just mentioned."

I know. But neither was Nicodemus, and Jesus told him, "You must be born again. I need to change your life. You need a new nature." And Nicodemus, who had assumed that knowing the doctrines equaled conversions, went away unconverted.

For three years he continued as a good church member, yet with a sense that something was wrong with him. He attended all the meetings, performed all his duties as a leader, but was empty and unhappy. Then one day the authorities arrested Jesus and took Him to Calvary where the Roman soldiers lifted Him up on the cross. In the crowd watching Him die stood Nicodemus. And when he saw Jesus, he remembered what Christ had told him: "Just as Moses lifted up the snake in the desert, so the Son of Man must be lifted up, that everyone who believes in him may have eternal life" (John 3:14, 15).

Nicodemus could not resist any longer. I imagine that he approached the cross, though to do so was a great risk. The Romans often executed anyone who showed any sympathy to a victim of crucifixion. Maybe Jesus' eyes met his, and he pleaded, "Please, Jesus; do not die without transforming my nature. Give me the new birth that You spoke of that night three years ago." Nicodemus was heard. Christ transformed his heart. And that timid man, who dared to see Jesus only in the darkness of night, now was not afraid to declare publicly that Christ was his Savior. And with Joseph of Arimathea he requested permission from Pilate to bury the body of Jesus (see John 19:38, 39).

The miracle of conversion happens. It may happen to you or to anyone who accepts it. All that it takes is to run to the cross of Jesus and acknowledge three facts:

First, we must acknowledge that we are sinners. The proud human heart finds nothing harder than to admit that it has not a weakness, not a personality problem, but sin. We can't blame our heredity, the environment in which we grew up, or even a lack of opportunities. Instead, we have to run to Christ and say: "Lord, help me, I am a sinner. I am the only one responsible for my actions, which sometimes I cannot explain, and I want to be forgiven."

Second, we must recognize that we can't do it by ourselves. While it is hard to admit, we simply cannot become good through our own efforts. Humanity drives itself crazy as it searches for self-control, mental strength, and the "good" it hopes to find in each one—all in an effort to gain salvation, when the true and only solution is to seek the Lord. We must look to Jesus, not to ourselves. Everyone must turn to Jesus and plead, "Lord, I have tried, but I can't! My nature leads me to sin. Please, help me."

Third, we must grasp the truth that God can transform and save us! Yes, my friend, God can! We have to look at Calvary and, like Nicodemus, fall at the foot of the cross and ask God to change the direction of our life—to give us a new nature.

The Word of God says that the miracle happens. It may even begin right now while you are holding this book. You may not feel it yet, but the Holy Spirit is working in your heart. Perhaps you may suddenly feel like closing the book and throwing it in the trash can because it makes you uncomfortable. The sinful nature can't stand what is right. But God's voice continues to speak to your heart. As you respond to it, you might wonder, *How can it be? How God can change my life in one second?* I do not know. Miracles are not explained, and conversion is a miracle.

I cannot explain how the water became wine in one second by the wonderful touch of Jesus. No chemist can account for it. As I said, we do not explain miracles—we accept them.

How was it possible for a man who was born blind to receive sight one second after Jesus' touch? No ophthalmologist can tell us. Again, miracles are not explained—they are only accepted.

Right now God wants to work a miracle within you—the miracle of conversion. I am praying while I write the final few words of this chapter—praying for you, with the assurance that you will say: "Lord, I accept the miracle."

Chapter Five

Is It Possible to Live With a Wolf?

Pastor, I do not think that I am converted. All the time I feel like doing what I should not do. My life is in constant conflict. I want to serve the Lord, but at the same time I want to do what is not right. Is there any solution for my problem?"

A 20-year-old man living in a very remote area raised the question, but a highly successful businessman could have equally asked the same thing. The problem is identical for man and woman, child and adult, rich and poor.

For some reason we've had the idea that when people become Christians they won't sin anymore—that they will now be perfect and good role models for others.

Why do Christians have more conflict in their lives than non-Christians?

First of all, we have to understand what happens the moment a conversion takes place. Many persons assume that God immediately removes our sinful nature, destroys it, and then places within our heart a new nature that delights in love and obedience. But that is not the case.

It would be wonderful if we would not desire to sin anymore and could live like Adam and Eve before the Fall. But God doesn't suddenly destroy the old nature. He places within the converted individual a new nature—that of Christ. But what happens to the old nature, the nature of the wolf? It stays there mortally wounded, but still alive. As the apostle Paul acknowledges: "Our old self was crucified with him" (Rom. 6:6). So now we have two natures—the one that Christ gave to us, as well as the old nature we were born with.

The ideal would be to have the old nature always "mortally wounded." Unfortunately, it simply does not work that way. To use the analogy that Paul employed, the first time that the old nature receives food, it will start to recuperate from its wound, and if it continues to receive more nourishment, it will eventually get well and will fight to expel the new nature from within us.

No wonder new converts encounter tension and conflict than in their lives. Converted individuals struggle with more conflict than the nonconverted. Are you surprised? Try to understand what I am saying. Yes, the person who accepts Christ can expect more conflict than before. They will wrestle with more temptation. And they can expect to find themselves plunged into despondency and despair—until they understand what is going on.

It is as simple as this. The individual without Christ has only one nature: the one they were born with—the nature that sins just as easily as water runs downhill. It has nothing to oppose it. There is no conflict.

But when you commit your life to Christ and experience the miracle of conversion, you now have a new nature that is in continual opposition to the old. Do you understand now why life may seem to run along so smoothly for the unconverted? They have only one nature, and it controls their lives unopposed. But not long after conversion, just when they think the old nature is dead and gone, they discover that it is still there, and the conflict starts.

The converted have two natures, and the two are in perpetual warfare with each other.

The apostle Paul experienced it, and there was a time in his life that he almost got into despair. He declared: "I do not understand what I do. For what I want to do I do not do, but what I hate I do. And if I do what I do not want to do, I agree that the law is good. As it is, it is no longer I myself who do it, but it is sin living in me. I know that nothing good lives in me, that is, in my sinful nature. For I have the desire to do what is good, but I cannot carry it out. For what I do is not the good I want to do; no, the evil I do not want to do—this I keep on doing. Now if I do what I do not want to do, it is no longer I who do it, but it is sin living in me that does it. So I find this law at work: When I want to do good, evil is right there with me. For in my inner being I delight in God's law; but I see another law at work in the members of my body, waging war against the law of my mind and making me a prisoner of the law of sin at work within my members" (Rom. 7:15-23).

Two natures—two powers—struggled for supremacy within the apostle Paul. It created a conflict that compelled him to exclaim in anguish, "What a wretched man I am! Who will rescue me from this body of death?" (verse 24).

Now, I ask you: When Paul wrote his letter to the Romans, was he converted or not? Surely he was. However, here is the experience of a converted person who feels the conflict produced by the two opposing natures.

Therefore, my friend, do not be discouraged because you find yourself torn by conflict after you become a Christian. You and I are individuals with two natures that do not like each other. The apostle Paul understood it one day, and he wrote: "So I say, live by the Spirit, and you will not gratify the desires of the sinful nature. For the sinful nature desires what is contrary to the Spirit, and the Spirit what is contrary to the sinful nature. They are in conflict with each other, so that you do not do what you want" (Gal. 5:16, 17).

"Pastor," you may ask, "do you mean that my whole life is going to be a life of struggle and conflict?" Not necessarily—it all depends on your decision. The two natures are fighting today, but eventually one nature or the other will win. One will gain control of your life, while the other will die. Which one will win? That also rests upon your decision.

Let me illustrate it this way. Suppose that in a circus arena two wild animals start fighting each other. Their trainers pull them apart and place each one in a different cage. One receives plenty of food and water. The other one gets almost forgotten, except for a few occasions that someone slips it a little bit of food, just enough so it will not die. And now in that condition the two creatures meet in combat again. Which one will win? Is there any doubt? You know that it is the one that has been fed.

This is what happens in the fight of the two natures seeking to control our lives. Only one will gain victory—doubtless the better nourished one. It happens that usually the sinful nature is fed more, and this is the cause of constant failure, even after conversion.

God works a miracle by implanting in us the new nature, but if we did not take care of it, if we do not feed it, the sinful nature will always be seizing control of us.

But how do we feed the two natures? Through the five senses. Everything that enters our mind through them is food for one or the other nature—especially that which comes through our sight and hearing. That is why we should be very careful in our choice of programs, films, magazines, and even conversation and music.

It is true that while we are in this world, one way or the other, even against our wishes, we will encounter some nourishment for the sinful nature. Sometimes we hear unsuitable music in a public place or see a bad image while watching the news. It is impossible not to hear negative talk while in school or on the streets. But I can avoid voluntarily putting such things in my mind. At times some crumbs will slip in to feed the sinful nature. But I do not have to stuff it with "steak."

In reality, our victory, and consequently our happiness in the Christian life, depend to a certain extent on the way that we learn to live with both natures. How? By feeding the new nature that Christ gave us and letting the sinful one starve. This is what Paul meant when he said: "Those who belong to Christ Jesus have crucified the sinful nature with its passions and desires" (verse 24).

At the time the apostle wrote it, whenever the authorities crucified individuals, society declared them legally dead, but many times the victims would linger on the cross for several days in suffering and agony. Sometimes relatives and friends would take them off the cross and care for them. Thus it was possible for some to survive and continue a life of crime and rebellion.

The apostle is saying that we should leave the old nature nailed on the cross—not take it down or feed it.

"Well, Pastor," you might say, "for how long will I have to live with that struggle between the two natures?"

While we remain in this world we will never get rid of the old nature completely. But we may lighten the battle by not feeding it. Although we can keep it "mortally wounded," it still will not go away. But thanks to God, we have a powerful promise: "I declare to you, brothers, that flesh and blood cannot inherit the kingdom of God, nor does the perishable inherit the imperishable. Listen, I tell you a mystery: We will not all sleep, but we will all be changed—in a flash, in the twinkling of an eye, at the last trumpet. For the trumpet will sound, the dead will be raised imperishable, and we will be changed. For the perishable must clothe itself with the imperishable, and the mortal with immortality. When the perishable has been clothed with the imperishable, and the mortal with immortality, then the saying that is written will come true: 'Death has been swallowed up in victory'" (1 Cor. 15:50-54).

Isn't that wonderful? A new body. No more sinful nature. Finally God will take away the old nature and will throw it out forever. Then we will have no more conflict, no more wish to sin. We will have only Christ's nature—a perfect nature that finds joy in love and obedience to God's ways.

Until then we have to learn how to live with the old nature, letting it starve to death and constantly nourishing the new nature. This is the secret that the apostle Paul discovered.

A few years after his letter to the Romans, Paul wrote to the Philippians: "Finally, brothers, whatever is true, whatever is noble, whatever is right, whatever is pure, whatever is lovely, whatever is admirable—if anything is excellent or praiseworthy—think about such things" (Phil. 4:8).

Did you notice that the apostle here speaks about supplying food for the new nature? He had discovered the secret for a victorious life. Not only did he not feed the old nature, but he let the new one take control of his life. "I have been crucified with Christ and I no longer live, but Christ lives in me" (Gal. 2:20).

And as the years went by, his old nature became weaker and weaker until just before his death he exclaimed that "the time has come for my departure. I have fought the good fight, I have finished the race, I have kept the faith. Now there is in store for me the crown of righteousness, which the Lord, the righteous Judge, will award to me on that day—and not only to me, but also to all who have longed for his appearing" (2 Tim. 4:7, 8).

"I overcame!" he declares. "I reached the goal!" I get excited when I think about his words. Does this mean that I also can overcome? Can I be victorious? Yes, my friend. You and I may. Christ guaranteed our victory on the cross of Calvary. He has promised to be always with you on your struggle. Whenever you think that everybody has forsaken you, that you will never make it, that you are a total failure, remember that He is near, loving, forgiving, and sustaining you. "For it is God who works in you to will and to act according to his good purpose" (Phil. 2:13).

It is only a matter of time until He will come and then the victory will be definite and eternal.

"God, thank You for the promise that one day the struggle will be over. Help me to feed the new nature and to let the sinful nature starve. I know that this is my part, O God, but even this I cannot do by myself. Please, do for me what I cannot do."

Chapter Six

Friends Defend Their Friends

We learned in the previous chapter that two natures fight within us, each seeking to assume control of our life. The devil will do all in his power for the sinful nature to win and to entangle us in a sinful life. His target is the mind—the will. The battlefield is the mind. If he conquers our mind, he has gained control of our lives. That is why he concentrates all his attacks on it. He will employ drugs, alcohol, cigarettes, sex, false theories—anything that will work. The method, time, or price is not important. His goal is to win the battle, to defeat and destroy us. You will find that the struggle is not easy, that sometimes you will feel like a frail desert bush trying to resist the howling blasts of a tornado.

Can we do anything about it? Does God have any solution? Yes! The apostle Paul says: "Finally, be strong in the Lord and in his mighty power. Put on the full armor of God so that you can take your stand against the devil's schemes. For our struggle is not against flesh and blood, but against the rulers, against the authorities, against the powers of this dark world and against the spiritual forces of evil in the heavenly realms" (Eph. 6:10-12).

As you see, we may have God's power. But the conflict will not cease, because our enemy is invisible, cunning, and persistent. He is also treacherous. Working under cover, often in disguise, he seeks to gain control of our life in a subtle way, often through temptation. And what is temptation? It is the total effort that the devil puts forth to induce us to sin. But temptation itself is not sin. You are not sinning because you are tempted to sin. If you are lying in your bed and a sinful thought creeps into your mind, you do not need to think that you are lost and feel guilt because a negative thought flashed through your mind for one or two seconds. As someone has said: "While you cannot avoid that the birds fly over your head, you can prevent them from building a nest there."

Temptations come in many forms. In fact, the devil has a big factory to produce them, each one carefully prepared to fit the individual. And the enemy knows the weak points of every human being. For some it might be alcohol, for others the use of drugs, and for another, misuse of sex. We struggle against a highly intelligent being who knows where we come from, the environment in which we grew up, and the character traits that we received from our parents. Doing everything possible to deceive us, he might hide behind sensual music, a beautiful girl, a handsome guy, or a fascinating philosophy. He will mask himself as an angel of light, if need be.

But all that he will do to deceive you is only temptation, and temptation, is not sin.

The enemy cannot make us sin against our will. The tempter can seek to trick us with bright lights, fame, money, glory—anything. But he cannot contaminate you against your will. If we fall into temptation, it is because we consented.

"However great the pressure brought to bear upon the soul, transgression is our own act. It is not in the power of earth or hell to compel anyone to do evil. Satan attacks us at our weak points, but we need not be overcome. However severe or unexpected the assault, God has provided help for us, and in His strength we may conquer" (*Patriarchs and Prophets*, p. 421).

We may illustrate the difference between sin and temptation with the telephone. Temptation is the telephone ringing. Sin happens if you answer. If you do not answer, there is no sin. Suppose the telephone keeps on ringing. Does it bother you? Sure. But it is only temptation.

Let us now consider some suggestions that might be helpful for us to resist temptation. When the temptation comes, try to think about something else. The battle is to occupy the mind. Therefore, fill your mind with biblical promises. A law in physics declares that only one object can occupy a space at one time. The space is our mind. It is empty only when we are sleeping. Every time a temptation surfaces, ask for divine help, sing a song, or repeat a Bible verse. If your mind is occupied with such things, it will have no space for anything else—in this case, temptation.

We cannot allow such thoughts or temptations to linger in our minds. To cherish them transforms them into sin. A sinful wish allowed to become a sinful act will, if repeated many times, become a vice.

Another fact that we would do well to remember is that the critical point of temptation does not last more than a few minutes. Remember the telephone illustration? If you do not answer it, it will eventually stop ringing. The good part of it is that after the temptation you may become stronger. Every time we encounter temptation we either lose or win, either conquer or are conquered. The response we give to the temptation will make us stronger or weaker. If we commit ourselves to Christ and overcome, we will be better prepared to meet the next temptation. But if we struggle alone and fail, we become weaker and more vulnerable when the next one shows up.

And now the most important counsel: do not depend upon yourself. Instead, depend on Jesus. This is basic, because the final result will depend on who occupies our thoughts. If we look to ourselves, our life will be a total failure. That is the human tragedy. Many people say: "Discover yourself, find your potential, explore your inner strength." But inside ourselves we find only anguish, emptiness, and many times despair.

God has a better way. He asks us to look at Jesus. It is the only safe way.

A story tells about the Indian fakir who came to a village declaring that he would demonstrate how to make gold. The villagers gathered around as he poured water into a huge cauldron, put some coloring matter into it, and began to repeat magic words as he stirred.

When he had their attention diverted for a moment, he let some gold nuggets slip into the water. Stirring a little more, he poured off the water, and there was the gold at the bottom of the cauldron.

The villagers' eyes bulged. The local moneylender offered 500 rupees for the formula, and the fakir sold it to him. "But," the fakir cautioned, "you must not think of the red-faced monkey as you stir. If you do, the gold will never come!"

The moneylender promised to remember that he was to forget. But try as hard as he might, the red-faced monkey sat on the edge of his mind, spoiling all his gold.

Does this sound familiar? The more we try to forget our errors, and the more we attempt to push aside temptation, the more it stays in our mind. Let Jesus occupy your whole mind with biblical promises.

I remember an experience that made a deep impression when I was 6 or 7 years old. The school had two big 16-year-old guys. One would slap the children and take things from them by force.

My mother used to give me 20 cents every day for a little snack. At that time 20 cents was enough to buy a strawberry ice cream and some toasted peanuts. Probably I was more interested in going to school for the ice cream than in actually learning anything. To a 6-year-old boy ice cream seemed the greatest thing in the world.

Once when I was on the way to school the bully approached me and demanded my money. Although I resisted, he twisted my arm and by force got my 20 cents.

"Do you see that guy without an arm?" he asked me later as he pointed to a one-armed boy who lived in the neighborhood. "Do you know why he has only one arm? I cut off the other one. And if you tell your mother or the teacher that I took your money, I will cut your arm off, too."

From then on my life became a nightmare. Every single day I had to give my money to him. The worst part of it was that I could not tell anyone. I did not want to lose my arm. Many nights I would cry while alone in my room. Sometimes during recess time the older boy would buy ice cream with my money and would eat it near me while laughing at me and making me miserable. What could a 6-year-old child do against a 16-year-old boy?

Then one day as I watched the children playing during recess time, the boy slapped a little one. At that very moment the other big guy in school came by and hit him. To my surprise the bully was not brave enough to confront someone his own size.

It was then that I had a bright idea. Going to the other 16-year-old, I asked, "Would you like to earn 10 cents every day?" And then I told him the whole story. He promised to protect me. We decided that the next day he would be waiting for me at the same place the bully stopped me every day.

That night I could hardly sleep. *Tomorrow,* I thought, *will be my great day. Never again will someone take away what belongs to me.*

Next morning I got up very early. Mother gave me the money, and I left for school. There on the usual place lurked the bully. I did not look at him, but he started after me anyway and demanded the money.

"Never again, did you hear? I am not going to give you my money anymore," I said, looking defiantly into his eyes.

Staring at me as if he could not believe what he had heard, he started to twist my arm. But at that moment my new friend came running from the other side of the street, and we "defeated" him.

Today I find the incident humorous, but I still tremble when I remember the many hours of anguish that as a 6-year-old child I had to endure.

We are the 6-year-old child, and the devil is that 16-year-old bully. Many times he comes and seizes not just ice cream but the joy of living itself. Destroying our most cherished dreams and spoiling our plans, he robs us of our moral values and our self-respect, and he takes away our peace and our self-control. Then he laughs, because he considers himself victorious. And his laughter is like a slap in the face of Jesus.

Sometimes he plays with us the way cats do with mice. For a time he ignores us until we think that we are free; then he again chases after us to hurt and humiliate us.

Why does it have to be that way?

On the other side of the street a God-man was hung on the cross, to give not only forgiveness but also power. When He died, the enemy thought that he had conquered, but on the third day a victorious Christ rose from the grave. Today He lives—lives to give us power. Look to the empty tomb. Look to heaven and see Him willing to fight for you. Christ conquered the enemy in the desert and on the cross. He defeated him when He died. Now He needs only to gain victory in our heart. The decision is ours. He can't overcome in our heart if we do not consent.

Our enemy is a conquered enemy, desperately fighting "like a roaring lion looking for someone to devour" (1 Peter 5:8), because his time is short and he knows that he is defeated.

A legend tells of a warrior fighting on the battlefield, whose head had been cut off. But he was so engrossed in the combat that even without his head he continued slaying his enemies, until someone looked at him and announced, "You do not have your head. You are dead." At that moment the warrior fell down.

It is like that, my friend. We are fighting against an enemy with the head cut off. Christ has already overcome him. Will He also overcome in your heart? You are never alone.

"Satan cannot endure to have his powerful rival appealed to, for he fears and trembles before His [Christ's] strength and majesty. At the sound of fervent prayer, Satan's whole host trembles.... And when angels, all-powerful, clothed with the armory of heaven, come to the help of the fainting, pursued soul, Satan and his host fall back, well knowing that their battle is lost" (*Messages to Young People*, p. 53).

"Cry unto the Lord, tempted soul. Cast yourself, helpless, unworthy, upon Jesus, and claim His very promise. The Lord will hear. He knows how strong are the inclinations of the natural heart, and He will help in every time of temptation" (*Messages to Young People,* p. 67).

Chapter Seven

Is It Possible to Be Perfect?

I met Ricardo in Victoria, Espirito Santo, Brazil, while I conducted a Week of Prayer. He came to see me at the hotel one night after I had preached about the two natures struggling in each believer.

"Pastor," he said, "somehow I think that God is not fair when He asks us to be perfect. He knows that we are born with a sinful nature and that it leads us to do what is wrong all the time. I already have done too many wrong things in my life! It is impossible to be perfect."

Before we can respond to his concern, we need to examine the life of some men whom God considered to be perfect.

The Bible declares of Enoch that he "walked with God; then he was no more, because God took him away" (Gen. 5:24). If God decides to bring someone to heaven, it is because the person is perfect, don't you think? But why did God take Enoch? The Bible answers: "Enoch walked with God."

Now consider Noah's case. Scripture says: "Noah was a righteous man, blameless among the people of his time, and he walked with God" (Gen. 6:9). Wouldn't it be wonderful if God could say about you, "This is a righteous, perfect man" or "This woman is perfect"? Isn't that what you are trying to be? But does the Bible consider Noah righteous or perfect? The Bible answers: "He walked with God."

The Bible describes Abraham as "the father of all who believe" (Rom. 4:11). Did you know that one day God approached him and said: "I am God Almighty; walk before me and be blameless" (Gen. 17:1). Notice the request. All that God wanted of Abraham was that he would walk with Him. The result would be a perfect life.

Scripture announced that God had "sought out a man after his own heart" (1 Sam. 13:14). Oh, if one day God could say the same about us! What else could we wish? But how did David become a man after God's own heart? What was his most desired goal? "That I may walk before the Lord in the land of the living" (Ps. 116:9).

Did you catch the phrase that Scripture applies to all these individuals? All were perfect, because they "walked with God." A wonderful relationship of love existed between them and God. In their experience they had come to the point that they could not live apart from Him. That's why the Lord considered them holy, just, and perfect.

But notice something else common in their lives. One day Noah drank so much wine that he took off his clothes, got naked, and embarrassed his whole family. Have you ever done something humiliating like that? Noah did, yet God said that he was just and perfect among his people.

Abraham was such a coward one day that he was afraid to admit that Sarah was his wife, instead claiming that she was just his sister, something that almost caused Pharaoh to commit adultery with her. The results would have been terrible if God had not intervened miraculously that night. Abraham was a coward. But God said that he was perfect.

And what about David? He plunged into the dirty waters of adultery and murder. Most of you have never gone that far! Yet God allowed the claim to remain in Scripture that the king was a man after God's own heart.

The Lord is trying to tell us something wonderful through the experience of all these individuals. Something that will change our life and will give us hope.

According to human standards an individual is perfect, holy, just, and upright, when he or she never makes a mistake but keeps all the laws and regulations.

God, however, regards a person as perfect when he or she is

willing to walk with Him. When Christ is the center of their lives. When they understand what Jesus did for them on the cross of Calvary and ask for a new heart capable of loving. When they feel sorry for all the suffering that they have caused to Jesus and love Him to the point of exclaiming: "O, Lord Jesus, I love You. Without You there is no meaning to my life. Help me to walk with You!"

At that moment God rejoices and holds their weak hands with His powerful ones. Their past is erased forever, whether they were alcoholics, cowards, adulterers, murderers, or anything else before then. All is buried. In its place Christ gives to them His victorious life and perfect character and takes upon Himself the punishment that they deserved because of their sins.

Then begins the most beautiful and wonderful experience of walking with Jesus.

It is obvious that love is vital in such an experience, because we cannot stay together and be happy with someone that we do not love.

Our tragedy is that many times we define perfection according to our capacity to obey the principles or rules of a church or of a book.

But God evaluates our perfection according to the relationship that we have with Him.

As we start walking with Jesus we immediately find many things that may appeal to us but that Christ does not like, because He knows they are not best for us. And also there are many things that Jesus likes but we do not. What shall we do under the circumstances?

Again love comes to solve the problem.

When I was a little boy, I did not like papaya. Several years later I met an extraordinary girl, who is my wife today. We started dating and after a time got married. I will never forget the first breakfast in our home. As I left the bedroom I saw the table specially decorated and in the center a big papaya. My wife stood by it with an inquisitive look, as if she were thinking, *I wonder if he will like it.* After we prayed, she cut the papaya into two pieces and gave one to me. As I looked at the fruit, then at her, I felt like saying, "Thank you, but I do not like papaya," but I couldn't. Loving her and not having the nerve to disappoint her, I took the fruit and practically swallowed it whole.

The next morning, as I left the bedroom, what I saw almost paralyzed me. There again was papaya on the center of the table. Glancing at my wife, I managed to say, "Looks as if you like papaya very much."

"To me, breakfast without papaya is no breakfast at all, my dear," she replied.

Instantly thoughts of eating papaya for the rest of my life raced through my mind. But when I looked at my wife and noticed that beautiful smile, I was happy too. I loved her. To eat papaya was nothing compared with the joy of seeing her happy.

When we fall in love with Jesus—when we love Him with our whole heart—above anything else we will like to see Him happy and smiling. Undoubtedly some of the things that will make Him happy we do not like to do. I do not believe that it will be easy for us to stop doing the things that we enjoy and learn to do some things that we did not enjoy till then. There will be a price for us to pay. It will require effort, sacrifice, and perhaps suffering, but it will be worthwhile if we do it because we love Jesus.

The prophet Micah explained the right way to walk with God. "He has showed you, O man, what is good. And what does the Lord require of you? To act justly and to love mercy and to walk humbly with your God" (Micah 6:8).

The issue is not only to walk with God. The important thing is to "walk humbly" with Him. The Leader, the one who shows the way, He knows what things are best for us. I love Him and accept His counsel because He knows what is good for me. I do not lead the way or take God where I think I should go. I just hold His hand and walk. He is my Father, my Friend, my Brother, the Alpha and Omega (the Beginning and the End). He is all. I trust in His love and go wherever

He wants me to go and do what He says. After all, He knows the way and above all wants me to be happy.

All this makes sense only in the context of love. The motive behind everything must be love for Jesus. If no relationship of love exists between Christ and us, life becomes empty and meaningless. Christianity becomes a heavy burden of prohibitions and duties. We may carry that burden one or two or 20 years, but one day we reach our limit or we become like robots, fulfilling our duties and obeying, but without joy, enthusiasm, or happiness.

Then one day, while with friends, someone may ask, "Why don't you drink?" And we may answer with embarrassment: "Because my religion forbids it. It is a rule of my church." Many times the whole life goes on like that. We do or don't do things because of our church or of our religion. But what about Christ? He knows what is best, but do we trust and love Him?

Let me give an example. One day I went with my wife to buy a pair of shoes for her. After looking at several pairs, she was undecided between two that she liked. She tried one and then the other. Suddenly she turned to me and asked, "Which ones do you like?"

"Listen," I said, "it really does not matter to me. You are the one who is going to wear the shoes. Take the pair that you like better."

"No," she said, "I want you to choose."

"Why?"

"Because I love you, and I will be happy wearing the shoes that you chose for me."

I was so touched that we bought both pairs.

That is exactly how our relationship should be with Jesus. We have to love Him in such a way that He becomes very real to us until we can look at Him and ask, "Do You like it? I will be happy to wear the clothes that You choose, because I love You."

To walk with God is to have Him present in our daily activities. It is to ask His counsel before we make a decision, before we date, before we put on some adornment, before we go to a program or any other place.

Our life is not limited to a church. The mere name of religion should not determine our actions. We do or we do not do; we eat or we do not eat; we wear something or we do not wear it, because we love Christ and trust Him. If we see a smile on His face, we keep on going. If, on the contrary, we see sadness, it is time to stop, not because the church prohibits something, but because we love Him and trust Him.

Now let us go back to the title of this chapter. Is it possible to be perfect? If you think that to be perfect is never to make a mistake, then it is impossible. But, thank God, the biblical concept of perfection is different. To be perfect in the sight of God is "to walk with Him" as did Enoch, Noah, Abraham, and David.

Have you ever seen a father walking while holding the hand of his 4-year-old son? The father's steps are big, and the child cannot keep up with him all the time. But the son grips his father's hand and keeps on going. Sometimes the boy may stumble, but as long as he holds his father's hand he will not fall. And what is the secret to continuing on? The father's hand. He is the sustainer, the only surety that in spite of any falls the boy will get there.

That's why Enoch, Noah, Abraham, and David were perfect. The first one held so tightly to the Father's arm that we do not have any record that he fell down even once. The other three walked with God, stumbled and fell, but kept on holding His arm. They got up and continued walking. And God considered them perfect.

Did you ever make a mistake? Don't despair. Look to the cross of Jesus. Having paid the price for you, He forgives and accepts you. Are you hurt? Was the fall so terrible that you do not have strength even to lift up your arm and ask for help? Again, don't worry. Just turn your face to the cross, on which a God of love is slowly dying. Why do you think He suffered this way? Because He loves and values you.

"Pastor," you may say, "it can't be true. He cannot forgive me. You speak like that because you do not know me." You are right. I do not know you, but I do know the love of God. One day when I was in great despair, He loved me, forgave me, and accepted me. For this reason I can say to you: Look to Jesus— "to him who is able to keep you from falling and to present you before his glorious presence without fault and with great joy" (Jude 24).

Chapter Eight

Friends Like to Communicate
With Each Other

A fter all," the letter read, "it seems that there is no solution to my case. I know that prayer would help me to solve the problem, but I do not feel like praying. The worst of it is that when I pray I say all that I have to say in two minutes. It seems as if my prayer does not go beyond the roof."

Did you ever have the same feeling? The years that I have been working with young people have taught me that their problem is not that they don't know that they need to pray. Everyone knows that prayer is a necessity, that it is food to sustain the new nature. That power comes through prayer. Their real problem we find expressed in the letter above: "I do not feel like praying. I know that I should pray, but I can't. What shall I do?"

In the first place, it is necessary to understand what prayer is. "Prayer," said Ellen G. White, "is the opening of the heart to God as to a friend" (*Steps to Christ,* p. 93). According to this statement prayer is nothing more than conversation with a friend. Friends like to talk, to communicate with each other. It is what they do most of the time. If someone does not feel like talking to a friend, it is not because he or she does not know that friends need to talk. Rather, the problem is with the relationship. Something is wrong. A barrier has risen. The friendship is shaken, and the solution does not consist in reading books or listening to sermons that emphasize the duty to talk with a friend. Instead, it is necessary to learn how to solve the problem with the friend—to restore the bonds. Once that problem has been dealt with, the dialogue will come spontaneously.

60

In the second place, we must remember that a good and sound conversation between friends has its basis in sincerity. A true relationship between friends allows no room for pretense or hypocrisy. It hurts enough when you find that anyone has been a hypocrite to you. But when that person is someone you love very much, the pain is far worse.

Christ loves us, and He expects that our relationship with Him will be above all an honest one, a fact that He emphasized in His sermon on the mount. "And when you pray, do not be like the hypocrites. . . . Do not keep on babbling like pagans" (Matt. 6:5-7).

The Greek word translated as "babbling" is *battologeo,* usually employed to express what the parrot or the drunken person does, such as talking and walking without thinking.

What Jesus is trying to tell us is that when we talk with Him we should be honest and should feel what we say. He wants our prayer to come from the heart and not only from the mouth.

When my youngest son was 5 years old, he did not like vegetables. Lumping all the green vegetables together under the label "plant," he would announce, "I do not like plants." One day, at dinner time, the table was filled with green vegetables. Immediately his smile vanished. We asked him to pray, and he offered the following prayer: "Father, I am upset. There are only 'plants' to eat."

Do you know how he would pray today as an adult? He would thank God for the delicious food on the table.

There is our problem—we are not honest. For example, when we get up in the morning, we thank God for "the good night of rest." Although we may have rolled about in bed a hundred times or perhaps woke up with back pain, we still say, "Thanks for the good night's rest."

We in effect have memorized one prayer for the mornings and another one for the evenings. Always the same words. Maybe we do not feel like praying at all, but because we have the habit we just repeat the usual words. It is no wonder that when we lie down we have the strange feeling that our prayer did not go above the roof.

Why don't we see prayer as a wonderful opportunity to talk with Jesus, instead of a daily duty?

Do you have friends? What do you talk with them about? Is it the same thing every day, or do you change the subject? Did you ever think about chatting with Christ? To talk with Him just for the pleasure of doing it? To pray only to tell what happened during the day, even the unimportant things?

The day that we discover the joy of talking thus with God, we will have uncovered the secret of a victorious life.

"But Pastor," you may say, "I do not want to talk with God." Then tell that fact to Him. Explain that you know you should pray but that you do not feel like it. A miracle will then happen, you can be sure. When you least expect it, you will find that you are talking with God, not for one or five minutes, but 20 or 30. And the most important fact is that the frustration that your prayer does not go above the roof will disappear, and you will experience the joy of talking to Jesus Christ as to a friend.

It would also be good to remember that we should not approach God only for spiritual matters. We have to include Him in our daily life—in our work, dates, school program, and the longings of our heart that we do not dare to tell anyone.

It may happen that we did something wrong during the day and in the evening we just repeat: "Lord, forgive my sins." How long does it take to repeat this sentence? But what if instead of just repeating "forgive my sins," we tell Him what really happened? All the details. Why not explain the struggle that we had before we gave in, and how we felt afterward, the lessons that we learned, what we want Him to change in us, and so on. We should take as much time as needed. Because we are not fulfilling a "hard duty," we should not hurry. After all, we are just talking to a friend, the most wonderful and compassionate friend that any human being can have.

And as time goes by and the friendship deepens, the praying time will become more pleasant and longer. Our trust in Him will increase to the point that we will have a personal relationship beyond the comprehension of those who do not experience the same thing.

Remember the story of Gideon? A man of prayer, he knew his divine Friend and talked with Him. One day he found himself in a very difficult situation that required a decision. Not knowing what to do, he went to the field and talked to his Friend. His Friend never had failed him before and certainly would not fail now. "Lord," he said, "I need a sign. I will put a fleece of wool on the floor; and if the dew be on the fleece only, and it be dry upon all the ground beside it, then I will know that You will save Israel through me, as You have promised" (see Judges 6:37).

And God, the friend, answered his request.

But Gideon was still not convinced. He tried God one more time. "Allow me one more test with the fleece. This time make the fleece dry and the ground covered with dew" (verse 39).

We may think that Gideon was playing with God, but he wasn't.

Gideon had a personal relationship with Him. They were friends.

At that time Gideon was just a scared and indecisive human being. He needed an indication, because he did not want to make a wrong decision. When he asked for it, his wonderful Friend answered.

"Pastor," you will say, "those things do not happen anymore today—only in Bible stories."

Does it need to be so? Our God has not changed since that time. He is the same and still wants to have a friendly relationship with each human being. All we need is to learn to talk and communicate with Him—to love Him and let Him embrace us with His arms of love.

When I was a student, I heard a story that I will never forget. It told of a young man whose greatest dream was to be a missionary in Africa. Five days before graduation the principal of the school announced that the General Conference had two openings for two young men willing to be missionaries in Africa. Extremely excited, the young man ran to get more information.

"Pastor, I would like to be one of those missionaries in Africa. This has always been my most cherished goal."

"Very well, my son," the administrator answered calmly. "The General Conference has four travel tickets available."

"Four? I heard that there were only two openings."

"Must be two couples, my son. We cannot send a single man to Africa."

The stipulation left the young man speechless. He was not engaged, nor did he have any girl in mind. And the plan was that they should leave right after graduation. "Can't they make an exception? It is impossible to find someone in such a short time."

"No, my friend, if you want to fulfill your dream, you must start looking for a wife right away."

Three days went by, and the young man had tried as hard as he could to go as a single missionary. When he finally perceived that the General Conference would not change its policy, he went to his room and prayed. He and Jesus were friends. They always talked. And at that crucial moment of his life, the Friend certainly would not fail.

"Dear Lord," he prayed. "You know that all my life I have wished to be a missionary in Africa. Here is my great opportunity, but I can't go there unmarried. I have to get married. If I choose in such a hurry, I might make a mistake. Therefore, I'm going to ask You something different, Lord, trusting in our friendship and in your wonderful love and with the certainty that You never fail. When the bell starts ringing for dinner, I will run to the cafeteria, get my tray, and sit at the table in the far corner. The first girl who sits down at the same table, I will believe, is the one that You are sending to be my wife. We will marry and go to Africa."

The bell rang. He raced to the cafeteria and the seat in the far corner. Silently he prayed once more. "Lord, it is Your turn now. Please send the right girl."

The students entered and chose tables. Finally one girl filled her tray and glanced around. Then she looked in the direction of the young man's table and started walking toward it. Spotting her, he started praying: "Lord, please, send any girl but this one." He had hardly finished when she arrived and, saying "Excuse me," sat down. A few minutes later other students joined them.

That dinner was the most terrible one he had ever had. He could not understand what was going on. The girl had always given him the impression that she was a snob. During their four years together in college they had never exchanged more than a few words.

When the meal was over, he approached her.

"I want you to answer just one question for me. You know that we are not friends and during the past four years we have never eaten together. Why did you come to the table where I was today?"

"I do not know," she answered. "I was getting ready for dinner, and all of a sudden I felt a strange sensation, sort of a conviction or voice telling me, 'As you go to the cafeteria, look for a table where there is a young man by himself, and sit there.' At first I paid no attention to it, but while I was coming, the voice continued, 'The young man who is alone, the young man who is alone.' And when I got my tray, I still heard that voice: 'The young man who is alone.' And the only one by himself was you."

It was unbelievable! The dew on the ground, and the dry fleece, do you remember?

The student looked into her eyes and said, "We have to get married right after graduation."

"Get married?" she replied, startled. "I do not want to get married to anyone, much less to you, and certainly not right after graduation."

But when he told the whole story, she became convinced that God was leading the circumstances and gently agreed, "Well, we shall get married."

Sounds like a fanciful novel, doesn't it? But that is the secret of a victorious life—the relationship that we have with Christ. We may relate to Him as to a name, a theory, or a doctrine. Or we may have the relationship of a friend.

"Pastor," you may ask, "do you mean that I may request a sign from God?" Not always. If He did not give clear and precise instructions in His Word, and if you are willing to humbly accept His counsel, and if you really can trust Him, then you may ask for one.

Not too long ago after I had preached a sermon on this subject, a young woman approached me and said, "Pastor, I am married to a man who is affiliated with another church, because when he asked to marry me I requested a sign from God, and He answered positively." Yet the Word of God clearly says: "Do not be yoked together with unbelievers" (2 Cor. 6:14). Therefore she had no need to ask for a sign. What would you think about a man who wants to rob a bank and asks God if he should do it or not? In the Bible the command "You shall not steal" (Ex. 20:15) is very clear. You have no need to ask for special guidance that ignores what is plain.

To pray is a great privilege for human beings. Opening the heart to God as to a friend, asking for counsel, or just talking is the type of prayer that strengthens the soul and feeds the new nature.

A story from the Vietnam War relates that someone found in the hands of a dead soldier a note written during the last agonizing moments of his life. "O God, I never talked with You before," it said. "Today for the first time, as I heard the noise of weapons and saw the bodies of my colleagues, and as I feel that in a little while I too am going to die, I wish to talk with You. It is too bad that now it is too late."

As did that soldier, perhaps we too have to say: "O God, I never really talked with You before, because all I did was repeat meaningless words, but today I truly want to open my heart to You and feel that You are my friend."

Chapter Nine

How to Feed the New Nature

Immediately after His baptism "Jesus was led by the Spirit into the desert" (Matt. 4:1). In that solitary region He pronounced words that will always be the key for a happy and victorious life. "Man does not live on bread alone, but on every word that comes from the mouth of God" (verse 4).

"Pastor," you may question, "I know that you will talk about Bible study and that I must read the Bible. But I do not want to read it—I do not like it."

In the first place, my friend, do not take Bible reading as a duty. Regard God's word as a love letter. How does a young man react when he receives a letter from his girlfriend? Would he grumble, "Oh, what a pain! I do not feel like reading it; I am tired, but I will take a look just to fulfill my duty"? Certainly not. What happens is just the opposite. He receives it with great expectation, opens it quickly, and devours each word. And does he throw it away? By no means. He keeps it in his pocket. Two minutes later he pulls it from his pocket and reads it again and again and again, until he has memorized it. But he still continues to read it.

Why such eagerness to read the letter? Why does he not get tired of doing it? The key word is "love." The young man loves the person who wrote the letter.

The Bible, my dear friend, instead of being just a code of rules and prohibitions, the history of a wandering people, or a textbook of ancient measures, names, colors, strange animals, and prophetic symbols, is rather the most beautiful love letter ever written. It is the story of an incomparable and profound love that we cannot under-

67

stand, a love that does not get tired of waiting. Scripture is a declaration of love written with the red ink of Jesus' blood. From Genesis to Revelation a red thread weaves through each page—the blood of the Lamb of God crying from Calvary: "My child, I love you—you are the most precious thing I have."

In the Bible you also find the stories of men and women just like you. People that faced conflicts and temptations and sometimes slipped and fell. Individuals that fought against their temperaments and passions, but overcame by the blood of the Lamb. By these stories God says to you: "Child, you will overcome. Do not give up. Instead, look forward and proceed."

But, as in all the other aspects of the Christian life, the great enemy is formality. A mechanical Bible reading is of very little value in feeding the new nature. Bible reading must be a time of fellowship and dialogue with its Author. As you read a verse and meditate upon it, try to apply its message to your life. Ask yourself: "What is this verse trying to tell me?" Then it is your turn to talk. Tell God what you think about the message and how it applies to your life. Do not be in a hurry. Enjoy each minute of your conversation with Jesus. Do not treat it as a duty or a heavy burden to carry, but rather as an opportunity to receive the wonderful promises of God to you.

Another interesting approach that will help you enjoy the Bible is to read it using "I" every time you see "we." Place your own life in the pages of the Bible. Pretend that God is talking to you in particular and not to humanity in general. For instance, Romans 8:31: "What, then, shall we say in response to this? If God is for us, who can be against us?" You may read: "What, then, shall I say to this? If God is for me, who can be against me?" Then you may tell God all those things that you think are against you, share the fears, doubts, and uncertainties that you struggle with, and then close by saying that in spite of all these things, you believe that if God is with you, nothing will prevail against you.

With these ideas in mind I want to share with you some practical suggestions that Pastor Tercio Sarli presents for a daily period of meditation, prayer, and Bible study:

1. Choose a particular time—as you have a specific time for your meals, so select a special time to be alone with God, to meditate, to pray, and to read the Bible. Did you know that every 24 hours you have available to you 96 periods of 15 minutes? Why don't you take two or three of them to commune with God daily?

2. Choose a place—the spot where you spend the time in communion with God should be a quiet one, without anything to distract you. It might be the living room, the bedroom, the office, or even outdoors under a tree or by the riverside, as Jesus chose many times. The important point is that the place be consistently the same, if possible, and that you feel comfortable there.

3. Try to relax—forget your concerns and spend the first few minutes in silent meditation, thus preparing your heart to commune with God. If an important aspect of your work occurs to you during your period of meditation, write it on a piece of paper, and it will stop distracting you.

4. Keep in mind the purpose of this time—you are there to meditate, to talk with God, to hear His voice, to pray. Do not allow something else to alter your plan. Do not use the time to prepare a Bible lesson, or even something to present at a church program. Such moments are dedicated to communion with God and nothing more.

5. Start with a word of prayer—talk to God without formalities. Invite Him to be with you during these moments of meditation, prayer, and Bible study.

6. Use your Bible—select a portion of God's Word and read it attentively, meditating on each phrase, and seek to hear the voice of God through your reading. The Holy Spirit might

reveal to you wonderful truths to the Christian life. If you prefer, you may start with the Gospels, reading a subject each day. You will be surprised to see how much you will discover. Have a notebook with you to write down all your new insights from the Sacred Book.

7. Use other devotional books—in addition to the Bible, you may also read other good books for meditation, such as *Steps to Christ, The Desire of Ages, Christ's Object Lessons,* and many others. It is important not to read too much, but to focus on a portion that is sufficient to feed your spiritual life. To meditate is to digest what you have read.

8. Take moments to pray—now you are ready to talk with God as to a friend. Tell Him everything that is important to you. Says Ellen G. White: "Keep your wants, your joys, your sorrows, your cares, and your fears before God. You cannot burden Him; you cannot weary Him. He who numbers the hairs of your head is not indifferent to the wants of His children. . . . His heart of love is touched by our sorrows and even by our utterances of them. Take to Him everything that perplexes the mind. Nothing is too great for Him to bear, for He holds up worlds. He rules over all the affairs of the universe. Nothing that in any way concerns our peace is too small for Him to notice" *(Steps to Christ,* p.100). Pray as much as you want.

9. Determine how much time you want to spend in communion—there is no one time that is right for everybody. Some start with 15 minutes a day and gradually increase it according to their capacity to meditate. The joy of this time is progressive. Ellen G. White says that it would be good for us to spend one hour each day meditating on Jesus' life and His teachings.

Now, just start and persevere. Do not get discouraged if occasionally some obstacle interferes with your plans. If it happens, start all over again. As a result you will feel the joy of salvation and will be glad to tell others about your faith and happiness, because "the heart that rests most fully upon Christ will be most earnest and active in labor for Him" *(Steps to Christ,* p. 71).

Promises for you:

When afflicted—Matt. 11:28, 29; Ps. 23:4; Ps. 121:1, 2; John 16:1-3.

When forsaken—Ps. 27:10; 34:6-8; 37:25; 57:1; Isa. 12:2; 35:4; Jer. 29:13.

When sick—Ps. 103:3; Jer. 17:14; Ps. 23:5; Isa. 54:7, 8; Rom. 8:18; 2 Cor. 12:9; Num. 6:24-26.

When lonely—Zeph. 3:17; Isa. 25:4; Ps. 145:18; Isa. 51:11; Ps. 34:8; John 14:16-18; Ps. 68:5; Gen. 28:15.

When anxious or concerned—Matt. 6:25-34; Ps. 37:5; 42:11; Luke 12:27-29; Ps. 118:5; Phil. 4:19.

When a loved one has died—1 Thess. 4:13-18; Matt. 5:4; John 5:25-28; 1 Cor. 15:51, 52; Rev. 21:4; 14:13; Isa. 25:8, 9.

When in need of peace—John 14:27; Isa. 26:3, 4: Phil. 4:4-7; Ps. 37:11; 119:165; Prov. 3:1, 2; Isa. 48:18; Rom. 5:1.

When sad—John 14:1-3; Ps. 42:11; 118:14; John 15:11; Rom. 15:13; Phil. 4:4; Isa. 35:10; 57:15.

When in danger—Ps. 91:1-16; Heb.13:6; Ps. 18:2; Prov. 18:10; Ps. 16:8; 23:4; 27:3; 34:7.

When afraid—Ps. 121:1-8; Heb. 13:6; Ps. 4:8; Luke 12:7; Ps. 27:1; Matt. 8:26; Ps. 27:3; 28:7; Isa. 43:1; 41:13.

When you have sinned—Ps. 32:1; 1 John 1:9; Ps. 103:3; Rom. 8:1; Ps. 103:10-13; Rom. 6:23; Isa. 1:18; John 3:16; Isa. 44:22.

When lost and without direction in life—Joshua 1:9; Jer. 6:16; Ps. 73:23, 24; Rom. 8:14; Ps. 32:8; John 16:13; Prov. 4:18.

When wishing for salvation—John 3:16; Acts 16:31; Heb. 9:28; Eph. 2:8; Rom. 6:22, 23; John 6:40; Ps. 62:1.

Chapter Ten

Would It Be Possible to Stay Quiet?

To be in love is a wonderful experience. Did you ever fall in love? Do you remember the day that you declared your love? Perhaps your hands were sweating, you were shaking, and you could not speak up. But you gathered enough courage and finally told the girl of your love for her. She looked at you with a bright countenance, and finally, when you thought that you would hear the dreamed-for yes, she with peculiar sweetness said that she needed a little time to think about it. Did that happen to you?

If so, you will never forget those days of expectation, and especially that day when she finally said yes. You were on cloud nine, and I am sure you felt like running to announce to everyone, "I am happy because she accepted me." When you got home, you took the phone and started calling all your friends: "I have good news—she loves me." Afterward you got your pen and some paper and wrote to your relatives: "Do you know that I am in love?" Unable to stay quiet, you had to tell everyone you knew. The joy of this love was such that if you did not tell others, it would "explode" in your heart.

But what would happen if you started dating a girl without loving her? Would you tell everyone, or would you keep it as a secret so that nobody would know of your relationship with her?

Something similar happens in our relationship with Jesus. The day that we will love Jesus with our whole heart we will wish to tell everybody about our relationship with Him. It is impossible to stay quiet. We will find ourselves driven to witness to others the wonderful news of salvation.

The Bible regards it as impossible for salvation and witness to exist apart from each other. The experience of salvation will necessarily take us to witnessing. Someone simply cannot be saved and not witness. The joy of salvation is so great that it produces in us the need to tell others what we are feeling.

When we talk about witnessing, we do not mean only to go from door to door distributing printed material or to conduct a series of meetings for 30 or more nights. Both are means of witnessing, but there are countless other ways.

Let us talk about the easiest one: friendship. We all have friends. At work, at school, in the neighborhood. Young people love to make new friends. They find them on the streets, at the bus stop, or in the restaurants. And the Bible says that friendship is an extraordinary means to witness.

Let us examine the experience of one of the first Christians.

Andrew accepted the "Lamb of God" when he heard John the Baptist. Immediately loving Jesus, Andrew accepted Him as his Lord and Savior and automatically became a witness. It could not have been otherwise. The first thing he did was to find someone to whom he could tell his great discovery. He sought out Simon, his brother (see John 1:40). Both fishermen, they worked together—a fact that reveals a vital element in the dynamic of witnessing. It is more effective to witness to people with whom we relate in our daily activities. Without any doubt the testimony of a friend is more powerful than that of a stranger.

Therefore, my dear reader, you may seek a friend in the neighborhood, or at work, or in school, and without formalities or hypocrisy tell him or her what Christ means to you, what He has brought to your life, how He helps you in your daily activities, and how He has given you peace. Do not worry about methods or theories. Just be a friend and introduce others to your friend Christ. Tell about practical things and also share with them how Jesus has changed the lives of other young people whom you know, such as those who were into drugs or struggled with despair, and to whom Jesus brought joy and happiness.

Invite your friend to your church. Introduce him to other friends in the church.

You may organize a group of young people to meet in one of your homes to study the Bible and pray together.

As you see, my dear young friend, all that you need to witness or to do missionary work, if you prefer to put it this way, is to have your heart so full of love for Jesus that it is impossible to keep it secret. Such love will compel you to witness.

Do not think of witnessing as something complicated. Just accept it as a privilege and as a means to feed your new spiritual nature, because every time you tell others about Jesus' love, that love will increase in your own heart. Every time you present Bible truths to a friend, those truths will become more real to you.

To witness is one of the secrets of keeping alive your own Christian experience. A story tells of a man who, while traveling on an extremely cold winter day, started to freeze without realizing it. He was to the point of giving up his struggle to stay alive when he heard the moaning of another traveler who was all but dead from the cold. The first man, his compassion awakened, decided to try to save the second man. First he started rubbing the dying individual's arms and legs until he could stand up. But the other man was too weak to walk. So the first man took him in his arms, and together they crossed territory that the first traveler had thought that he could never traverse by himself.

After he had taken the fellow to safety, suddenly it occurred to him that by saving the dying man he had also saved himself. His vigorous efforts to massage the other man had stimulated his own circulation, bringing warmth to his numb members.

A few years ago I read a story of a doctor who once found a small dog with a broken leg by the roadside. Sorry for the animal, he took the little fellow home, cleaned him up, set the broken bone, and put a splint on it to hold it in place.

The dog loved the doctor and followed the kind man around the house and yard until the leg was well. Then suddenly he disappeared. *That's gratitude for you,* the doctor thought to himself. *As long as he needed me, he stayed. As soon as he didn't, he ran away.*

But the very next day the doctor heard a scratching at the back door. When he opened it, there was the little dog. Back again, wagging his tail. Beside him, however, sat another little dog. And that dog was lame!

Yes, that's what happens in the life of someone who finds Jesus and loves Him. It is impossible to stay quiet. The joy is so great that the only way is to share with others what Jesus has done for us. Are you ready to witness?

Chapter Eleven

More Than Friends

We said in a preceding chapter that to be perfect is to "walk with God." He regards us as perfect and just, not because we have never sinned, but because we walk humbly with Christ. Many might think: *How is it possible to walk with Jesus if He is not here? We can't see Him or touch Him.*

It is true that Jesus is not here with us. He is in the heavenly sanctuary interceding for us. Intercession and judgment are works that need to be done. But at the same time, He wants to walk with us in this earth. He longs to take our hand and guide us through life, because He knows that it is very hard to live in this world. We need someone to help us and to give us power to overcome. What could He do? As the time of His death approached Christ gathered His disciples and said: "But I tell you the truth: It is for your good that I am going away. Unless I go away, the Counselor will not come to you. . . . But when he, the Spirit of truth, comes, he will guide you into all truth" (John 16:7-13).

The Holy Spirit is Christ's representative now.

He comes to comfort, to sustain, and to guide. To walk with God, then, in reality means to walk with the Holy Spirit. To walk with Jesus every day in a love relationship is nothing more than to allow the Holy Spirit to lead us.

Perhaps you have tended to regard the Holy Spirit as a power, something without life and sort of floating in the air. At least that's what I thought when I was a child. My mother used to pray "O God, fill us with Your Holy Spirit," and I imagined something intangible filling me. It took me several years to understand that the

Holy Spirit is a person. He is God—as much God as the Father and God the Son, Jesus Christ. The Spirit is a person who can know (1 Cor. 2:11); who has wishes (verse 11); who loves (Rom. 15:30); and who feels sad (Eph. 4:30).

When Jesus went back to heaven, He sent the Holy Spirit not only to walk with us, but to abide in us. "Don't you know that you yourselves are God's temple and that God's Spirit lives in you?" (1 Cor. 3:16).

Here we find a most intimate relationship. There should be no separation between us and the Holy Spirit. He wants to dwell in us.

It is by accepting His presence in our heart that we walk with God. It allows Him to occupy each little corner of our being. Because the Holy Spirit is His representative, the Spirit is Christ in us. Having taken human nature, all that Christ could do was for a time to be at our side. But, represented by the Holy Spirit, He transcends matter and space and abides in us.

The Holy Spirit is our most urgent need today. When we give Him the keys to our heart and allow Him to possess each inch of our being, it will change our lives as dramatically as what happens to the desert after a torrential rain.

Withered lives will flourish. People whose life has been a total failure will be victorious, The unproductive will become productive. Sad and discouraged hearts will again have joy and hope. Those filled by the Holy Spirit will overcome vices and break bad habits. The voice of the Holy Spirit is the shout of independence and the song of victory.

If we listen to the constant entreaties of the Holy Spirit, we will not run the risk of doing wrong. "Whether you turn to the right or to the left, your ears will hear a voice behind you, saying, 'This is the way; walk in it'" (Isa. 30:21).

The success of our lives will depend on whether we heed that voice. It will be there speaking to our hearts all the time. Comforting us when we are sad, encouraging us when we are afraid, clarifying things when we have doubts, giving counsel when we face the danger of straying from the right path.

That is how we walk with God. And that is how we are perfect, just, and good. To listen to the voice of the Holy Spirit, who speaks to us through our conscience, is to hold on to the powerful arm of Christ and to walk with Him.

Now let us consider a highly sensitive subject: The sin against the Holy Spirit. What exactly is it? One of the fundamental Bible doctrines is that of forgiveness. Christ died for us and through His death paid the price for our sins. If we accept Him as our Savior, He blots out our transgressions. It does not matter how we lived in the past or how deep we have fallen into sin. The Word of God declares: "If we confess our sins, he is faithful and just and will forgive us our sins" (1 John 1:9).

But the Bible warns us that there is one sin that not even God can forgive (see Matthew 12:34). Again, what is the sin against the Holy Spirit? Why can't God forgive it? How can anyone know if he or she has committed that terrible sin?

Let me illustrate. College-age Louis, a born-again Christian, is an active and devoted member of his church. One day his non-church member friends invite him for a birthday party on Sabbath afternoon. At first he answers no. But a few days go by, and his friends insist, "Oh, come on, there is nothing wrong with that." And to complicate matters, a girl whom he especially likes will be there. Finally the day arrives. In the morning he goes to church. After lunch his struggle intensifies. Two voices argue back and forth in his heart. One says go, while the other urges him not to. He does not know what to do. At that moment the telephone rings. It is that special girl.

"Hi, Louis, you are not going to let me down, are you?"

So he attends the party. On his way he hears very clearly: "Louis, you should not go. Today is the Lord's day, when He especially wants to be with you. That party will not have the kind of atmosphere you need to enjoy His company today." It is the voice of the Holy Spirit speaking to the heart.

Finally he arrives at the party. A number of things taking place at it disturb him and make him uncomfortable. The voice continues to whisper in his mind. Finally he decides to go home as soon as possible. Once he's in his bedroom he thinks about what he has done. "Why, Louis?" the voice gently asks. "You have ignored your Best Friend most of the afternoon." Louis promises never to do it again.

Time goes by. Then his friends invite him to a picnic on Sabbath at a place that will be filled with noisy secular activity. Again a struggle rages in his heart. One voice says: "Go ahead, Louis. It's not that much different from that birthday party." Another voice pleads: "Don't go, Louis. Remember how it bothered you last time?"

On the way to the picnic area the voice continues in his heart. "Louis, you should be in church today." But he tries to focus his mind on other things. At the picnic the young people sing and play a few games, and afterward start dancing and drinking beer. Louis can't participate in all of this. At least not this time. He does not drink.

But as additional time passes, he participates in parties and other entertainments more and more often. The voice of the Holy Spirit always speaks to his heart—pleading and counseling—but Louis tries to ignore it. What he does not notice is that after a time the voice speaks less and less, until finally it stops altogether.

Every time he receives a new invitation to some secular activity, he responds more readily. The voice has become silent. Now Louis not only goes but also actively participates—he smokes tobacco and drinks alcohol. Nothing disturbs him—nothing hurts his conscience. He does not wait for an invitation but seeks them out.

No longer going to church, he has started to justify his behavior. Defensively he protests that the church members are too narrow-minded. Soon he rationalizes that it all depends on how you look at things.

Where is that voice that he heard so clearly the first time his friends invited him to the party? Why has the voice of the Holy Spirit vanished?

The heart, my friend, is like the palm of the hand. If you are not used to hard work, and one day you hoe the garden, your hand will hurt. Should you stop, your skin will continue smooth and sensitive. But if you continue working in spite of the pain, you will see a red spot, then some liquid in it, and after a time the skin will become thicker and your hand will be calloused. You will not feel any more pain.

The pain that we feel when we start going the wrong way results from the voice of the Holy Spirit. But if we do not listen to that voice, the pain will decrease until the heart becomes calloused. Not only will the pain vanish; we will lose all sensitivity to wrong. That is what the Bible calls the sin against the Holy Spirit.

And why can't God forgive it? Is it because we have so offended Him that He does not care for us anymore? No, God's love is infinite, mysterious, and beyond understanding. Regardless of our mistakes—our rebelliousness against His voice—He still loves us. But why does He not forgive the sin against the Holy Spirit? It is not because He does not want to forgive, but because those who have come to this point no longer feel their error. Everything and anything now seems right to them. Nothing hurts anymore. They do not perceive God's voice pleading in their heart. Sin has anesthetized their lives, and they see no need to repent. Why? Because they do not think that they are wrong. As a result, they do not ask forgiveness, because they do not see any need for it. And God does not force humanity to accept His forgiveness. The sin against the Holy Spirit is unforgiveable, not because God does not want to forgive, but because human beings refuse to accept forgiveness.

Maybe at this moment you are thinking, *Could it be that I have offended God's Holy Spirit? Is it possible that He spoke to me and I continued doing the wrong thing? What do I do if for that reason the Holy Spirit is not speaking to me as before?*

When I was a missionary among the Campas Indians in the Amazon region of my native country, I went through an experience that taught me a great lesson. Forced to spend the night in the jungle, I decided to make a bonfire. Fire means life to the Indians. With it they prepare their food during the day, and at night it is light, protection, and warmth.

"Pastor," the Indians had told me, "at night in the forest, make a bonfire. It will provide heat and will repel wild animals and insects."

Remembering that suggestion, I gathered dry wood and arranged it the way that hunters do to cook and to provide heat and light. I had learned all this in a Pathfinder leadership class. But when I looked for the matches in my backpack, I discovered to my shock that the box had gotten totally wet. As I struck the matches one by one, they refused to light. By now I had begun to get frightened. All I had left were five or six, and if not even one of them worked, I would have to spend the night in a dark and unknown forest. Just the thought of it made me tremble. I knew what that meant. Desperately I tried to remember all I had learned about starting a fire. I looked for an empty bird's nest. Usually they caught fire easily. There one was! As I struck two more matches the flame snuffed out as before. Removing my shirt, I hung it up on one side to shelter any fire from the wind.

It is now, I thought. *It must be now.*

One more spark. I blew softly to see if it would ignite the sticks and dry grass. But nothing happened.

"It has to be now, or never!" I trembled as I prayed to God.

The tiny flame was right there in the dry nest. Carefully I blew until a small stick burst into flame. I placed a piece of straw over it and blew again. A dry leaf. One more straw. A tiny fire glowed in the nest. I kept on blowing. One more leaf; one more straw; a little stick, then a larger one. Soon the fire was burning. I thanked God I would not spend the night in the cold. I had light. I had heat. I was safe!

Sometimes we start drifting from God. We go far away from the Father, the church, the family, and even ourselves. There, in that distant land of anguish, despair, and loneliness, we find ourselves abandoned and distressed. And in that condition we cry: "Is there hope for me, Lord?" And Jesus answers, "Yes, there is, My dear son or daughter. I always loved you. My Spirit was always with you. Come back to My loving care."

At this moment it is possible that the voice of God is blazing within your own heart like a big bonfire. If this is the case, be grateful to God and ask Him to continue to guide your life. It is also possible that the voice of God might have become just a small spark. Please do not let it extinguish. But what will happen if the voice of the Holy Spirit in your life is nothing more than a little spark? Please, keep it going. Don't let it die. Obey it. Let it guide your life and listen to it. At the beginning it will be just a small fire, but if you continue listening to it and obeying it, soon that voice will be like a raging bonfire.

The fire of the Spirit is our guarantee of victory. The Holy Spirit will finish in your life the redemption work started by Jesus. To be full of the Spirit means to be guided by His voice. It means to heed His counsel and orientation. Are we willing to do it?

Chapter Twelve

To Know Jesus Is All

The question of the rich young ruler, "What shall I do to have eternal life?" is the question that beats in the heart of humanity. God created human beings to live. It is His greatest goal. Life might be miserable, but when death comes, human beings still cling desperately to it. Death is an unwelcome intruder. The most cherished desire of every person is to live. To hold to life, people will pay any price, make any sacrifice. "What shall I do to have eternal life?" is the desperate cry of the human heart. And Jesus' answer is simple: "Now this is eternal life: that they may know you, the only true God, and Jesus Christ, whom you have sent" (John 17:3).

Thus the secret of eternal life does not consist in the knowledge of a body of doctrines or in accepting a particular church. Rather, it is to know one person—the wonderful person of Jesus Christ. True Christianity is the relationship of two people: a human being and Jesus Christ. What matters in our spiritual experience is not *what* we believe but in *whom* we believe.

The reason to believe that true Christianity is a personal relationship between Christ and human beings is that justice and sin can exist only between people. A star, a cat, a table, or a stone cannot sin; neither can they be just. Only people sin. Therefore sin is more than a violation of a law—it is the breaking of a love relationship between Christ and humanity. Here we see the true picture of sin. When I sin I hurt my Lord, I hurt myself, and I create separation between us.

That Adam hid from God reveals more clearly the true nature of sin than just the fact that he ate the forbidden fruit. This is the worst aspect of it. The human being that once would go running to his Creator's arms now after sinning hides himself from fear, thus causing a deep hurt in God's heart. Was God sad because someone broke the law? Or was He suffering because of the separation it caused?

This forces us to conclude that salvation—eternal life— is a reconciliation with or a new relationship with the Lord of salvation. We are saved when we trust in Jesus and when we love Him, not when we believe in doctrines or join a church.

However, we cannot love someone without knowing them. Therefore, the devil will do all he can to separate us from God, or to lead us to approach Him with a wrong idea of who or how He is. The enemy does not want us to know Jesus, or if he cannot succeed in that, he will trick us into having a wrong picture of God, convincing us that He is arbitrary, severe, revengeful, and more concerned with regulations than with His children themselves. Such a picture of God does not produce love—it creates only fear. It makes us willing to serve Him not from love but rather as servants, those who only fulfill a duty or obligation. Consequently religion becomes boring—a formal Christianity. Fear of punishment compels us to obey. And Satan is quite happy with such a response. He has accomplished what he wanted. Although he might not have been able to keep us away from God, he brought us to Him for the wrong motives.

To know Jesus is all. Do you know why? Because in reality to know Him is to know what He did for us on the cross of Calvary. When we finally grasp the reality that He loves us in spite of our failures, we can't help loving Him with all our heart. And because we love Him, we will wish to be like what He is, to live in such a way that will bring happiness to Him, and to do what He wants us to do.

To know Jesus is all, because salvation is not a result of human effort but a gift from God, and this gift is Jesus Himself. Salvation does not come *from* Jesus—salvation *is* Jesus. Thus to accept salvation is to accept Jesus. And to know Jesus is to have salvation, and therefore eternal life.

When John says "to know Jesus," he is not talking about theoretical knowledge. The disciple lived in a time when Hellenistic thought predominated. The Greeks greatly valued theoretical knowledge. For a Greek to say that he or she knew a flower, they would go to the library, study what all the books had to say about that flower, and then would declare: "I know that flower." John was different. For him to declare that he knew a flower meant that besides reading the books, he would go to the fields, see the flower, touch it with his hands, smell it, and feel it. Only then could he claim: "I know the flower."

To know for John, the beloved disciple, was to have a personal experience. Theoretical knowledge may help when everything is normal. Experimental knowledge, on the other hand, is the only solution when there is a crisis.

Most of the disciples limited themselves just to hearing Jesus' words. John went a little further. He liked to stay close to Jesus and to recline his head on Jesus' bosom (John 13:23). The difference that made manifested itself when a crisis arose. When the Jewish authorities arrested Jesus, all the disciples fled Him. The only one who remained anywhere nearby was the one who not only heard Jesus, not only sought to know about Him, but obtained an experimental knowledge (John 19:26, 27).

"Now this is eternal life: that they may know you, the only true God, and Jesus Christ, whom you have sent." We humans sometimes complicate things and make them difficult, robbing them of their natural beauty.

This little book, my dear friend, has sought to show you as simply and clearly as possible the whole process of conversion and Christian life: justification, imputed righteousness, sanctification, and glorification.

"But I did not find these words as I read it," you might protest. And you are right. I did not mention them even once. I am sure you have heard them many times before, but it seems that they have not helped a lot. I wanted to present the same truths in a different manner.

In the first chapter, for instance, I mentioned the story of the rich young ruler—a very sad example of those who seek righteousness through their own efforts. The result is a meaningless and empty life. My own experience when I was young echoed that of the young ruler. In the third chapter I tried to explain in an uncomplicated way the profound theme of forgiveness, atonement, and justification. What Jesus did for us on the cross is not only liberation from guilt, but also substitution. Someone paid the price for our sins. He was treated as we deserved, so that we may be treated as He deserves. Because He took our place, we now may have His. Jesus offers to us His merits, His righteousness. Christ took our sins and paid their price on the cross. As we look to that cross and see the Son of God dying for us, we find ourselves drawn to Him. We are reconciled and justified by Him and receive a new nature, something that we call imputed righteousness.

But why after we have been justified and reconciled do we still have the desire to sin? It is then that the two natures come into consideration. We have to feed the new nature through prayer, Bible study, and witnessing; and we have to let the old nature starve to death. In other words, we have to walk with God as did Enoch, Noah, Abraham, and David—in a love relationship. This is sanctification.

However, the struggle will continue till Jesus comes. Only then will another miracle happen. God will then remove the old nature and throw it away. The struggle will be over. We term this glorification.

But until the Lord does return, we must continue with our lives, and the Lord Jesus helps us through the presence of the Holy Spirit. This is righteousness communicated.

As you see, in this little book we were not concerned with terminology. Wanting to be understood, I tried to show more practical things than just theory. I was not concerned with *what*, but *how*. But all this is meaningless without the *who*. He is the main character of this book, and He will have to be the main person in our lives if we want to live a successful and happy Christian experience.

I will never forget the emotion that I felt as I read about an incident that occurred in the United States. Thirty-six children found themselves trapped in a classroom on the second floor of a burning school in the center of Chicago. Those able to get out did so. But flames and smoke filled the stairway and blocked the emergency exits. Thirty-six scared little faces were glued to the windows. The firefighters had not yet arrived. Rescue seemed impossible.

Mark Spencer lived two blocks down the street. When he saw the fire, he ran to the school. His job that morning was not that of a police officer or of a firefighter. Something else compelled him. When he reached the school, he shouted to the children to break the windows. Pieces of glass flew to the ground. Mark was a tall and strong man. Everybody could see the confidence in his eyes and the strength of his arms and hear the love in his voice as he called to the children, "Jump, I will catch you."

One by one the children started jumping. His strong arms caught them and gently placed them on the ground. Finally all were safe— all but one. Little Mike stared down at the ground, then turned away. Mark screamed, pleaded, ordered: "Jump, I will hold you. Nothing will happen."

The boy's teacher ordered, "Jump, Mike, jump."

His 35 classmates added their voices. "Jump, Mike. We made it. You will make it too."

But the boy was frozen with fear. The next day they found his burned body. The body of Mike, son of Mark Spencer.

Why did the child not jump? We do not know. Nobody will ever know, including Mark Spencer. A loving father, he had given to his son all that he needed. He had played with him, shared his own heart. At the moment that Mike's life was at risk, Mark was there with open arms, pleading, imploring, supplicating to his son to jump, not onto the cold and hard concrete, but into his strong, safe, and loving arms.

But something went wrong. Mike died. Are we going to be different? Will we joyfully run to the arms of our loving and wonderful Father and walk with Him in a loving relationship, or as with little Mike, are we going to freeze with fear because the fires of formality have made us to see a distorted picture of God? to view Him as revengeful, cruel, and arbitrary?

The only way we can make the right decision is to come to know Jesus. Then we will not hesitate to leap into His arms.

You've read the greatest story ever told— but never quite like this.

Written in modern language without the disjointed interruption of chapter or verse, Jack Blanco's fresh, unified narrative merges the four Gospel accounts into one. No long genealogical lists. No confusing, archaic words. Just the timeless story of Jesus, our Saviour. Paperback, 160 pages

3 WAYS TO SHOP

- **Visit your local Adventist Book Center®**
- **Call 1-800-765-6955**
- **Online at AdventistBookCenter.com**

Availability subject to change.

FINALLY,
A BIBLICAL MODEL
FOR HEALING
THE MIND.

SATISFYING THE LONGING OF YOUR SOUL

Hunger reveals how you can truly encounter God and have a close relationship with Him. You'll discover the joy and fulfillment of such spiritual practices as simplicity, solitude, worship, community, and fasting. With fresh insight and practical guidance Jon L. Dybdahl leads you on a journey that will satisfy the longing of your soul. Paperback. 144 pages.

3 WAYS TO SHOP

- Visit your local ABC
- Call 1-800-765-6955
- www.AdventistBookCenter.com